I firmly believe that music will someday become a 'universal language.' But it will not become so as long as our musical vision is limited to the output of four European countries between 1700 and 1900. The first step in the right direction is to view the music of all peoples and periods without prejudice of any kind....

—*Percy Grainger, composer/ethnomusicologist, 1933*

The chief function of music is to involve people in life. Music is the thing that lets us go beyond culture, i.e. music is the vehicle for transcendence.

—*John Blacking, anthropologist*

Cultural variety lies under threat of extinction. A grey-out is in progress which, if it continues unchecked, will fill our human skies with the smog of the phoney and cut the families of men off from a vision of their own cultural constellations.

—*Alan Lomax, folklorist/ethnomusicologist, 1977*

Environmentalists are telling us that we're losing 15,000 species of plants and animals every year, but how many languages are we losing? And with them, how many myths and stories? How many songs and instruments?

—*Steven Feld, anthropologist/ethnomusicologist, 1993*

SONGCATCHERS

IN SEARCH OF THE WORLD'S MUSIC

mickey hart

WITH K.M. KOSTYAL

NATIONAL GEOGRAPHIC

Washington, D.C.

[PRECEDING PAGES] Balinese dancers performing with a gamelan orchestra

[BELOW] Mickey Hart with Gyuto Tantric Choir, whose chants he has released on a number of albums

[RIGHT] A turn-of-the-century photograph showing a very early use of sound with projected images

private ritual, and I didn't want anyone making fun of these sounds or the life I shared with my newfound friends. I was a shy kid and these African troubadours were my companions. I was as free as a bird when I soared with this music, and any bullies who might be waiting for me just outside my living room door could not get into this world.

This music made me powerful, and even though the singing was in a language I didn't understand, I was getting it. I was receiving its message, and it made me feel special. Who were these people, and why me? I wondered. Was anybody else listening? In fanciful moments, I had an image of all the people on my block huddled next to their record players doing the same thing, hoarding their own musical treasures and not telling anyone. But eventually I would snap out of it and realize that this wonderful music was my secret alone.

At the same time that I was being transported to the world of the Pygmies, another phenomenon was sweeping the streets of New York. It was the mid-1950s, and the city was turning on to the music of Cuba and Puerto Rico. This Latin music, derived from African sources, had become dance and trance music in the Caribbean. The islands brought together Hispanic, Native American, European, and African sounds in a whole new way. African American bandleaders like Dizzy Gillespie were invigorating jazz with Latin rhythms and instruments. Fifties dance crazes made mambo, guaguanco, cha-cha, and rhumba into familiar middle-class terms. Masters like timbalero Tito Puente and the great bandleader Machito were combining this Latin music with the hot brass and syncopation of the city to form a new gumbo, a spicy stew that would send us all into ecstasy.

The throb of this steamy, polyrhythmic music was in the air. After-hours clubs that specialized in Latin music were springing up around the city. Everyone—black, white, Hispanic—was listening. Many New York teens were casting off the ropes that bound them to the old '50s swing music of their parents. The new music was made for dance and romance—and dance was the new currency of the street. This sound-feeling would bring folks together like nothing else had before. It would meld politics, race, and religion into one seething, gyrating mass of humanity, and we would dance our way through the '50s and into the next stage of the American adventure.

Elsewhere around the country other teens were turning on to this music. Musicians like Elvis Presley, Chuck Berry, and Ritchie Valens combined R & B and country music to create rock and roll. Young white Americans learned to dance with a new, free abandon.

If music tells the story of who we are, then this was the soundtrack of American possibilities, and it pointed the way to who we really could be, not who our parents and grandparents were or what had moved them. We had equity in this music, it was

The dancing went on late into the night at New York clubs in the 1940s and '50s. [LEFT AND BELOW]The Latin beat in the city grew stronger, as dynamos like Tito Puente [OPPOSITE] burst onto the scene. Harlem born but with Puerto Rico in his blood, the "sultan of salsa" picked up the tempo with his Latin jazz.

ours. It was a wellspring of creative forces at work, all around us, heard everywhere.

This was the new America, driven by a new beat—fast, hard, moving with such intensity that only a scream could describe it. After an hour or so of dancing to this wild new music, all you could do was yell, "Yeah, yeah, more, more, more." Everybody was out dancing, and seeing adults and teens dancing on the same floor, dancing for the sheer joy of it, was a new thing for me. We would visit our neighbors just to dance with them. The music let us kids be with our parents in a new way: No one told us how to dance or when. For me, the music worked to break down barriers of generation and class. It was a powerful glue in my community, a deep-down magic.

Stationed in Spain, the U.S. airmen also known as Joe and the Jaguars, with Mickey Hart on the drums, shook up the clubs in Madrid with their American rock.

[OPPOSITE] A National Living Treasure in India and a living legend throughout the world, Ali Akbar Khan influenced musicians from many different traditions with his mastery of the sarode, a 25-string instrument. Western violin master Yehudi Menuhin called him "the greatest musician in the world."

Ten years later, I had made my way to the far side of the continent, to San Francisco, and I was pushing the envelope myself with a band called the Grateful Dead. I had known since I was a kid that I wanted to be a drummer, and now I was one. But I had never thought about recording other people's sounds myself. Then, one day, my compadre in the Grateful Dead, rhythm guitarist Bob Weir, happened to suggest that we go down to the zoo in San Francisco and record the animals. There was a full moon, and in Weir's mind it was the perfect time to commune with the outdoors. The adventure of sneaking into the zoo at night and getting high with nature was irresistible. I borrowed a Nagra tape recorder and we approached the gates of the zoo.

The zoo run was a disaster. In our amateur zeal, we had needlessly packed a hundred feet of microphone cable for a four-foot job; it loaded us down and we got stuck on the gate. Our panic alerted the guards, who came running at the sight of intruders. Our adventure ended quickly. Still, that day marked a new beginning for me. The idea and excitement of capturing ambient sounds in a high-quality format caught my imagination. Though the zoo trip was unsuccessful, I saw the unlimited potential of recording, not just making, music. I remembered listening to the Pygmies, but their forest soundscape had little detail. Now, with modern-day equipment, the possibilities for accurate remote recording of music from all over the world were endless. Since I had a steady day job with the Grateful Dead, I could devote my free time to my newfound recording passion. Later, as the Grateful Dead's popularity and the Dead Head community grew, I was able to

> "As a drummer, rhythm is my god. The movement in things, the motion, the ebb and flow, the clickety-clack of life." —*Mickey Hart*

incorporate aspects of the world's musics into the band's vocabulary. I was also able to use my position in the pop music world to expose a broader audience to rare and amazing recordings by publishing my own series of CDs on Rykodisc.

In 1967 Phil Lesh, the bassist for the Grateful Dead, handed me a recording, *Drums of North and South India*. He said, "You've got to hear this, you won't believe it." I was astounded by the beauty and complexity of the North Indian classical rhythms. This music was crying out to be recorded, using world-class technology, by someone who really loved these sounds and the emotional payload that they delivered. The LP that Phil passed to me casually that night would be the catalyst for this book.

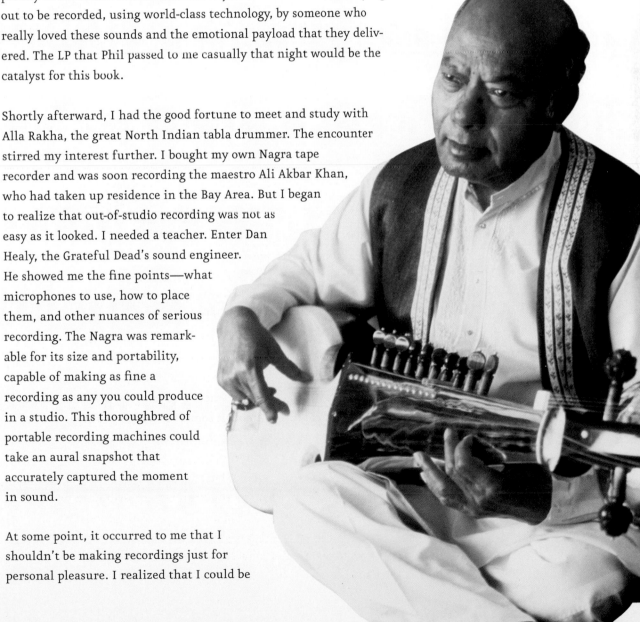

Shortly afterward, I had the good fortune to meet and study with Alla Rakha, the great North Indian tabla drummer. The encounter stirred my interest further. I bought my own Nagra tape recorder and was soon recording the maestro Ali Akbar Khan, who had taken up residence in the Bay Area. But I began to realize that out-of-studio recording was not as easy as it looked. I needed a teacher. Enter Dan Healy, the Grateful Dead's sound engineer. He showed me the fine points—what microphones to use, how to place them, and other nuances of serious recording. The Nagra was remarkable for its size and portability, capable of making as fine a recording as any you could produce in a studio. This thoroughbred of portable recording machines could take an aural snapshot that accurately captured the moment in sound.

At some point, it occurred to me that I shouldn't be making recordings just for personal pleasure. I realized that I could be witnessing the highest level of a vanishing art form. The modern world and its pop culture might make Ali Akbar Khan the last of his kind. The preservation of his music should go beyond my own lust for the sound: If I loved this music, sooner or later, the rest of the world would, too.

Since those days I've expanded my search for the world's music. I've recorded North African music, the gamelan music of Bali, the classical taiko drumming of Japan, Latvian choral music, American roots music, Dixieland, the shamanic music of the Arctic, Native American drumming and singing, the gospel songs of born-again felons, and the celestial chanting of Buddhist monks. I've learned what it takes to be a field recordist: how you have to fight the rain, the insects, the sand, the sun. You have to drink with and eat the food of the musicians you're recording and observe their traditions, no matter what they are. To understand the heart and soul of a music, to earn the right to hear it, you must respect and honor the culture that creates it.

At first glance, the story of field recording seems a simple one: men and women on the trail of the sounds we make. The story of why we make sounds—musical sounds—and of the machines we've invented to capture these sounds and of the songcatchers who traveled far and wide in search of them always held my imagination.

The more I recorded, the more I understood how hard it must have been for the early recordists. They didn't have Nagras or today's lightweight DAT recorders. Many of those turn-of-the-century songcatchers were women, making their way into an alien world. I began to see myself as a modern extension of this community—without having paid the dues they did. I had a great machine, and a mission to record.

Like those early recordists, I've come to understand the importance of safeguarding the world's music. This is the story of my search, my personal investigation into the adventures of the people who recorded and preserved that music. They brought this treasure to a wider world. When I learned about the difficulties and hardships these songcatchers faced, I realized the importance of protecting what they brought back and of taking this music seriously. I became an activist, without losing my sense of what is realistically possible. Not all musics of all traditional cultures can be recorded and documented before they become

extinct. Not all field recordings in the world's archives can be digitized before the media are lost forever. I hope this book will serve as a wake-up call to all of you about the importance of preserving the world's music.

Songcatching is not easy. It takes artists who create music and have the ability to turn a thought into a sound. It takes listeners who appreciate and support music. It takes technology to record and preserve that music. And it takes recordists who are willing to travel, sometimes to the remote corners of the Earth, to make sure the music is preserved. This book is about all those things and at the heart of it all, it's about the magic of music.

Ultimate power drummers, the Kodo group is devoted to "exploring the limitless possibilities of the traditional Japanese drum, the taiko." Since its 1981 debut, Kodo—a word that can mean both "heartbeat" and "children of the drum"—has traveled the world with music that critics praise as "primal power," "primitive, muscular endurance," and "visual sound."

I / why music?

What is music? At its most basic level, it is simply vibrating air, air waves in motion that the listener perceives as sound. But the skilled and caring use of these sound waves brings us nearer to the edge of magic. Music connects us with the soul.

Music expresses who we truly are and links us with the infinite universe; it is the orphan echo of the Big Bang that blew us into existence. It gives shape to our thoughts and feelings, things we can't express in words, turning spirit into sound. Music is the path the spirit travels between the physical and metaphysical worlds.

Before humans were painting the walls of caves, we were making music. Scholars believe that some early musical instruments may have grown from the act of toolmaking. From toolmaking, early humans could have moved to musicmaking, using seedpods, gourds, naturally hollowed logs, and animal jawbones. The water-carrying vessel, struck for resonance, became a water drum; the hunting bow was transformed into a musical bow that hummed with its own soft sound. The evolution of the brain and of the vocal apparatus are closely linked, and, if music and timbre gave way to language and speech, it is because rhythmic vocalization—solo or group—was a great evolutionary step in making the mind-body connection real. Anthropologist John Blacking even speculated that music, as an organizer of movement and sound, is one of the factors that helped the human brain develop into the kind of brain it did. Rhythmic movement, dance, and music, he thought, were actions that defined the human species.

About 15,000 B.C., a prehistoric artist painted a figure on the wall of the cave system known as Les Trois Frères, in southern France.

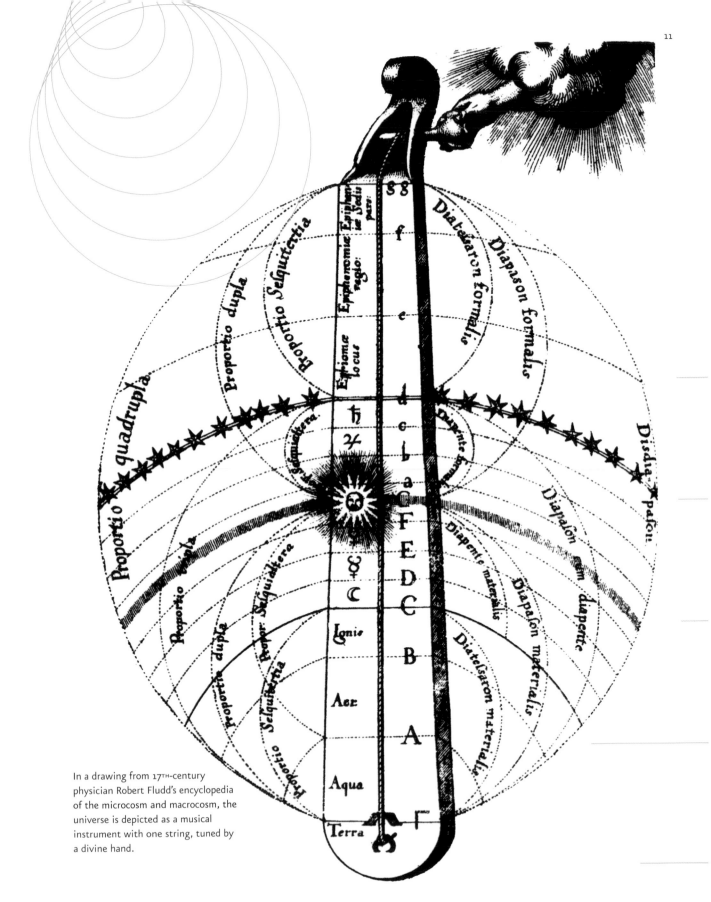

In a drawing from 17ᵀᴴ-century physician Robert Fludd's encyclopedia of the microcosm and macrocosm, the universe is depicted as a musical instrument with one string, tuned by a divine hand.

Some call it the "animal charmer" or "dancing sorcerer." Exactly what the figure is doing is unclear, but perhaps he was entraining with—joining in the rhythm—of the great herds, trying to make contact with them and their spirit world through music, through sound, through vibration. But who knows what he represented to his own people: a hunter-gatherer foretelling the great hunt? A shaman communing with his animal totem? Whatever he was, music may have been a crucial part of his power.

As civilization took hold in the Fertile Crescent, at the eastern end of the Mediterranean, a kind of music developed that would lead the way to the sounds of Western music in the present day. By 4000 B.C., the ever inventive Egyptians had harps and flutes, probably to entertain the upper classes. But they also used music to organize the communal labor of a group into a rhythmic, coordinated endeavor. By 3000 B.C., the Egyptians had developed a concept of musical intervals—fourths, fifths, and octaves.

"Let there be singing and music before you," extolled an Ancient Egyptian lyric. In a relief from Egypt's Valley of the Kings, a musician strums a harp while acrobats perform. A prized instrument, the harp was initially patterned after the hunting bow, becoming larger and more elaborate as the centuries progressed.

Thousands of years ago, the energy behind music was probably a key element in ritual and trance. In Sumeria, ancient documents refer to music used specifically for religious purposes. To the later nomadic Bedouin, forever wandering the desert, music had definite magical power. The Bedouins' *sha'ir*, their feared and respected poet musician, was more than an artist; he was believed to be possessed of supernatural powers.

In the East, music developed along other lines. In the 6TH and early 5TH centuries B.C., the Chinese thinker Confucius taught a philosophy based on order and harmony in all things—ethics, politics, daily living. He saw music as an integral part of his philosophy, a necessity in a well-ordered moral universe—and a thing of immense power.

"Correct" music was in harmony with the universe itself and brought order to the earthly plane. Those in government had to understand music in order to govern well. "When good music prevails, there is no

[BELOW] Singing colossus, a 65-foot-high statue of Egypt's great pharaoh Amenhotep III—one of a pair left standing near the pharaoh's tomb at Luxor—began to reverberate with a bell-like sound after an earthquake in 27 B.C. Greeks renamed it the "singing Memnon," in honor of one of their own heroes.

[RIGHT] Ever concerned with the afterlife, Egyptians often placed clappers, like the hand-shaped ones here, in tombs to scare off the evil spirits who were easily frightened by noise.

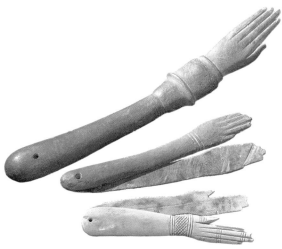

"What we call music in our everyday language is only a miniature, which our intelligence has grasped from the music or harmony of the whole universe that is working behind everything and is the source and origin of nature. It is because of this that the wise of all ages have considered music to be a sacred art." —Inayat Khan, Sufi mystic

feeling of dissatisfaction and when proper rituals prevail, there is no strife or struggle," Confucius declared. In his very specific way, Confucius even set down the six emotions portrayed by music—sorrow, satisfaction, joy, anger, piety, and love. Everyday language could not truly convey these emotions, he said, but music was its own kind of speech.

In Chinese tradition, the number five had cosmic meaning. All life resulted from the interaction of the five elements: metal, wood, water, fire, and earth. There were also five major colors, five flavors, five directions (center was the fifth)—and five main notes in the Chinese musical scale. Even before the time of Confucius, the Chinese used an

"Music rises from the human heart when the human heart is touched by the external world …. When the emotions are touched, they are expressed in sounds, and when the sounds take definite forms, we have music…. Music illustrates the primordial forces of nature." —*Confucius*

array of musical instruments: strings, winds, bells, and drums. They also had strict rules about how these were to be played. Jamming, as we know it, was not something Confucius valued in his well-ordered world. "When lewd, exciting and upsetting music prevails, we know that the people are immoral," he warned.

At about the same time, Greek philosophers were developing similar theories and drawing similar conclusions. The mathematician and mystic Pythagoras, born about 569 B.C., came to believe that numbers were the key to the universe. Since the attributes and ratios of musical scales are expressible in numbers, he concluded that the entire cosmos could be seen as "a harmony and a number."

Pythagoras had discovered, probably by measuring the lengths of vibrating strings, that the main intervals in music can be described in simple numerical ratios: the octave as 2:1, the 5TH as 3:2, and the 4TH as 4:3. Two millennia earlier Egyptians and Babylonians had made the same connection between intonation and numbers and had developed elaborate tuning systems. Still, Pythagoras' seven-tone scale would influence Western music for centuries to come.

Pythagoras also recognized the healing powers of music: music as medicine. He surmised that music traveled through the senses, affecting the body directly. Hearing beautiful melodies and powerful rhythms brought remedies to the soul. Different tones affected human behavior positively or negatively. Music could evoke sorrow or joy, courage or fear, compassion or anger. Pythagoras also believed that the revolving spheres that made up the heavens could be described, and heard, as musical sounds and intervals.

Though Pythagoras was a mystic and visionary, the thought of him actually hearing the music of the spheres is hard to grasp. Did he hear the music in his head? Was it mystical flight? A holy choir resonating in his brain? Maybe all of the above. Whatever he meant, his ideas on music are still discussed by scholars today.

A hundred years after Pythagoras, about 450 B.C., Plato approached music from a more philosophical, less mystical standpoint. Like Confucius, he thought music had a powerful role to play in human affairs, and because of that, it needed to be regulated. By using a system of notes and scales, the intoxicating or sensuous effects of music could be controlled. If rhythms or melodies were too complex, they could actually lead, he believed, to depression or emotional instability. On the other hand, if properly played, music could echo the divine harmony, the movements of heavenly bodies, and the moral order of the universe. In his *Republic*, Plato argued that the state should be based on the foundation of music—played properly. If musical traditions changed, he warned, the state could actually fall. Both Plato and Confucius understood the force that music carried: its ability to empower, to free the listener and the performer from time, pain, even space. Like the Greek concept of the muse, from which it took its name, music came from a realm beyond the mundane.

[ABOVE] Sixth-century B.C. Greek philosopher Pythagoras believed that musical harmony embodied the harmony of the cosmos, a word he is credited with originating. He is also credited with discovering the diatonic scale on the strings of his monochord. Many centuries later, the English poet Keats lionized the "World-famous golden-thighed Pythagoras" who "Fingered upon a fiddle-stick or strings/ What a star sang and careless Muses heard."

[OPPOSITE] At least 3,000 years old, a Shang Dynasty bronze drum, inscribed with animal, cloud, and thunder patterns, is a work of art in itself.

"It is not easy to determine the nature of music or why anyone should have a knowledge of it." —*Aristotle*

Despite some inherent harmonic problems, the diatonic scale held sway in the West until the Middle Ages settled on Europe. Then, in the seventeenth century, a new musical tradition—the baroque—emerged in the music of northern Europe and signaled a shift in what the ear found lovely. Elaborate harmonies and flourishes took the place of the mathematical intervals that had been so beloved in the diatonic system. Europe, with its new tempered scale, used baroque music as a tool of the sacred, something controlled by the church—by authority, just as Confucius and Plato had said it should be.

In a Persian miniature, Greek philosopher Plato quiets wild animals with music. As Hellenic civilization spread through the Mediterranean and into Asia, Greek ideals of harmony in music, governance, art, and architecture came to influence other cultures and would continue to do so for centuries to come.

To the east, meanwhile, a new religion had been creating a whirlwind that would blow musical trade winds across continents. Islam, founded by an Arab trader named Muhammad in the seventh century A.D., had swept out of Arabia to engulf most of North Africa and the Middle East. In the 11th century, Arab conquerors reached India, while tribes of the Asian steppes moved east in the 1200s. Musical traditions and instruments of the Middle East cross-pollinated with those of the Far East, and hybrid musics began to emerge.

Music, maybe because it is so inherent to human expression, always had a life of its own in the secular world, in impromptu dance, in the songs that a mother hums to her child or workers use to give a rhythm to their labor. But listening to performances of music for their own sake, apart from religious ritual or storytelling, is a relatively new thing in human history. The first opera house opened in Venice in 1637; about a half century later, the first public concerts for which admission was charged were held in London. Now the public could enjoy the "art music" that for centuries had only graced the ear of royalty and the high-born.

To musicologists, "art music" refers to a specific tradition, in which the musician is a professional expected to perform a given repertoire with a high standard of excellence. Western classical music, the court musics of China or Africa, the ragas of north India—these are examples of art music. They're not "back-porch music," the folk music of a small, isolated Alpine village, or the rhythms of a rain forest village in New Guinea. But these musics—sometimes called ethnic music, indigenous

Unharmonized Gregorian chants—or plainsong—were named for the late sixth-century pope of the Roman Catholic Church, Gregory I, who codified church music and gave it a place in the liturgy. Though sacred music has moved far beyond plainsong, for most Christian faiths song remains a prominent part of worship.

music, roots music, or world music, is as expressive and complex as art music.

In the last century, technology has allowed the musical trade winds to blow even harder, and the fusing of different musical traditions has happened very quickly. Classical concert musicians appropriated appealing aspects of the world's music. Popular musicians, like Elvis Presley and the Beatles, used "race music"— African–American dance/trance beats and Delta blues, both derived from music of the African Diaspora—to create the rock 'n roll that defined Western pop music for a decade.

Across all societies, the sounds of the natural world often influence music. Anthropologist Steven Feld, working with the Kaluli people in New Guinea, found that rain forest sounds would join with Kaluli music and mythos to create one glorious profusion of life sound. American rap music works the same way. It takes the sounds and the emotions of the city—the fears, the hopes, the dreams, the loves, and the losses—and mirrors them in the music. There is no silence in the streets of the city. It's a noise-filled, man-made forest of brick, pavement, and machines, all interacting in an incredible dance.

Modern classical composers have also appropriated new sounds into their work, and in fact the blurring of lines between sound and music is one of the most important changes to Western music in the past century. Noisemaking instruments freed composers who were already hearing the sounds of the city in their subconscious. These musicians changed the standard perceptions of music and musical instruments. Twentieth-century composers began to use unconventional forms of percussion, industrial noises, sirens, and eventually electronic center of the area that handles memory and emotions. That discovery has helped lay to rest a question that has nagged scientists about the processing of language versus music: Does the brain use the same processing system for both? It seems it does not. Music apparently has its own special corner.

Other studies show that a musician's brain is different from other brains, with a greater link between the two hemispheres and more gray matter in the area that processes hearing. Even age-old theories, like Pythagoras's ideas about the impact of harmony on the emotions, are now being put to the test of science—and it looks like they'll hold up. One scholar, Hajime Fukui, even tested the impact of music on testosterone production in the body and found that, in males, music suppressed it and in females, music elevated it—both conditions that would help humans get along together. To him, music may have been an evolutionary necessity for human society: "Music and certain sounds function to ease tension or strain, strengthen social bonds, bring pleasure or ecstasy, and bring cohesiveness among people."

"Music does not seem to be a mere game for the mind, for the neurons, or for the senses. Music seems to serve needs that are so important to humans that their brain has dedicated some neural space to its processing. It remains to demonstrate that these music-specific networks are fulfilling needs that are not optional but that have adaptive value." —*Psychologist Isabelle Peretz*

Most musicians don't spend their time worrying about the science of mental music processing. And for most, protecting traditional music is not a priority. We musicians want to make music—and will quickly learn how to speak music with anyone who wants to speak with us. Musicians are happy to jam with other musicians from any culture—as long as the results are musically satisfying. Yet thanks to my early interests in recording, and with the help of musical scholars of many stripes, I've spent the last several decades of my life—both as a musician and as a preservationist—loving, exploring, championing world musics, and trying to perpetuate them. As composer Lou Harrison urged, "Cherish, conserve, consider, create." Like the kind of music I make myself, traditional musics are full of movement, dance, poetry, ritual, and magic. These are some of the reasons that music has been a universal in human experience.

2 / songprints

It was, as always, the best of times and the worst of times—
depending on who you were. By the 1880s, America had finally knit
itself back together after a disfiguring civil war. For some Americans,
things were booming. But for plenty of others, times were tough.

Tough for African Americans whose new freedom had come with a new kind of enslavement and despair. Tough for the millions of European and Chinese immigrants who struggled to build lives in the face of prejudice. And certainly tough for Native Americans—the ones, that is, who had managed to survive the genocidal Indian campaigns of the 1860s and 1870s.

Those wars may have guaranteed the nation's Manifest Destiny and made the West a wide-open frontier for settlers and railroad barons, but they pushed the native cultures that had flourished in the West for centuries to the brink of extinction. Many were tribes that had already been herded up and moved once before, often thousands of miles from their homelands, to what the government called reservations. Some Plains Indians had landed in the canyon country of the Southwest; Appalachian Mountain Cherokee wound up in the arid sweeps of Indian Territory (now Oklahoma). But the displacements were just one aspect of a many-pronged program for the "savages." The younger generations were to be poured into the American mold. Government officials took Indian children from their parents and shipped them off to boarding schools, where they were "cleansed" of their traditional beliefs, languages, and customs—in short, their Indian souls.

In their attempts to subdue other cultures, 19TH-century Americans may have been trying to exert some control over a world that was rapidly

> 1856

Edouard Leon Scott de Martinville's phonautograph incises vibrations into lampblack but has no playback mechanism.

appreciation. In Paris, officials at the 1889 Universal Exposition named Edison the "inventor of the age."

Meanwhile, Edison was touting his talking machine to American scientists. Taking it to Washington, D.C., he did a test demonstration at the National Academy of Sciences in 1878. Several people in the audience fainted when they heard the recorded voice, others vomited, and one observer called the situation "diabolical." Clearly, the phonograph would take some getting used to.

One of the most prominent people in the audience that day was physicist Joseph Henry, head of both the National Academy and the fledgling Smithsonian, an institution he had stalwartly committed to scientific research of all kinds—including the social sciences. A year after Edison's diabolical demonstration, Henry's Smithsonian acquired a new, Congressionally mandated bureau—the Bureau of Ethnology (later the Bureau of American Ethnology).

Ethnology, or cultural anthropology—the science of studying human cultures, languages, and artifacts—came into its own in the second half of the 19TH century. For decades, a handful of Americans had understood that the cultures of Native Americans were disappearing and that their traditions needed to be documented for scientific posterity. In upper Michigan, an Indian agent and amateur ethnologist named Henry Rowe Schoolcraft had begun a serious study of Ojibway culture, trying to preserve its nuances before its people were assimilated into the voracious white culture. And in the 1860s, one-armed Civil War hero and Grand Canyon explorer John Wesley Powell came to appreciate the ways of the Indians he encountered on his far-reaching Rocky Mountain Expedition. Powell reported glowingly of a West where "men are not crowded against one another. The land is yet broad enough for all." Except the Indians. Powell recognized that the settlement of the West could be the death knell of the native peoples.

It was through the force of Powell's personality and lobbying that the Bureau of Ethnology had come into being. For the rest of the 19TH century he would be the prime mover behind anthropology in America.

"There is no great and uninhabited region to which the Indian can be sent. He is among us, and we must either protect him or destroy him." —*John Wesley Powell*

Like other ethnologists, Powell was particularly committed to "salvage" anthropology—documenting Indian languages, beliefs, customs, and artifacts before they disappeared. Languages interested him especially, because they could be compared to one another to trace a kind of evolution of civilization. But studying language was a time-consuming proposition, requiring tedious handwritten transcriptions of strange sounds that often had little in common with the sounds of English. For some reason, it apparently never occurred to Powell that there was now a machine to do some of that work, and do it better than a human could.

That thought did occur, though, to Harvard naturalist Jesse Walter Fewkes. Fewkes later wrote that, while in the Southwest, a visit to the Zuni "in the summer of 1889, had inspired in me a wish to attempt to record on the cylinders of the songs, rituals, and prayers used by these people, especially in those most immutable of all observances, sacred ceremonials."

Fewkes had visited the Zuni at the behest of Mary Hemenway, a Boston blueblood with a hobbyist's love of anthropology and the money to fund her own South-Western Archaeological Expedition. The expedition leader, the colorful and controversial Frank Hamilton Cushing, had first gone out to the pueblos as a Bureau of Ethnology employee. But Cushing was no bureaucrat, and he had produced very little in the way of written reports. Still, he had "gone native"—the eastern press called him the "White Indian"—and penetrated Zuni culture to the extent that he was initiated into the secret Order of the Bow. As sickly as he was sensitive, Cushing couldn't take the harsh conditions of fieldwork for too long. By 1889, Mary Hemenway was looking for his replacement. The buttoned-down Fewkes was her choice.

About as far from Cushing in personality as possible, Fewkes roused the ire of his predecessor and other anthropologists already on the South-Western Expedition. One of them called him "the Codfish." Reserved he may have been, but Fewkes was about to change the world of anthropology—and of songcatching—forever.

Before heading west, Fewkes made a quick trip north in mid-March 1890 to Calais, Maine. At the outskirts of town, a settlement called the Camps was home to one of three remaining bands of Passamaquoddy, "the purest blooded Indians now living in New England," Fewkes felt.

[OPPOSITE, TOP] Harvard zoologist Jesse Walter Fewkes, a student of famous naturalist Louis Agassiz, would change the course of American anthropology by introducing the phonograph as a tool for recording oral traditions.

[OPPOSITE, BOTTOM] By the time Fewkes took his phonograph to the Zuni in the early 1890s, the sacred ceremonies of Pueblo Indians had become mere curiousities to white onlookers.

"In sacred observances, it is probable that the music of the songs preserves its character even after other parts have been greatly modified."

—Jesse Walter Fewkes

On March 15, he began making what would become the first field recordings. He worked with Noel Josephs and Peter Selmore, Passamaquoddies who knew the old oral traditions. Over the course of a few days Fewkes recorded 36 wax cylinders of their songs, folktales, vocabularies, and conversations. Josephs told Fewkes at one point that he could remember when the songs and dances of the Passamaquoddy were performed in a large wigwam. By 1890, that image already conjured a lost world.

The machine Fewkes used in 1890 had much greater fidelity than the device on which Edison had recited "Mary had a little lamb" a dozen years before. But even that first Edison device had predecessors. Twenty years before Edison, in 1856, Edouard Leon Scott de Martinville had created a machine that scribed sound into lampblack smeared on a drum. The problem was that Scott's "phonautograph" had no mechanism for playback. A French inventor named Charles Cros had also succeeded in transcribing sound, but it was Edison, backed by talented technicians and his own commercial savvy, who brought sound recording from the world of the experimental to the realm of the practical, and profitable.

In introducing his talking machine, Edison touched off a competitive maelstrom. A few years after the original Edison phonograph appeared on the market, Alexander Graham Bell put his own technicians, Charles Tainter and Chichester Bell (a cousin), to work creating a new, improved version. They were the ones who replaced tinfoil with wax-coated, cardboard cylinders, creating and marketing something they called a graphophone. In 1887, Émile Berliner, a German immigrant, went a step further, developing a flat disc on which to record. Though his gramophone was still a work in progress when Fewkes recorded the Passamaquoddy, it would eventually revolutionize recording.

> **1887**

American Oberlin Smith invents a process for making magnetic recordings on steel wire.

"In acoustic recording, you have to move a lot of air to make the diaphragm move, in turn to make the stylus engrave on the wax. For a recording pioneer like Fewkes, the only way he'd know he was actually getting sound was to see if the embossing point was making a steady scarp in the wax. He probably had to make dozens of recordings to get a few good ones." —*Neil Maken, recording preservationist*

Noel Josephs, a Passamaquoddy man, became famous as the first voice ever captured on a field recording. When Jesse Fewkes made the recording in March 1890, in Calais, Maine, he could see that, among Joseph's people, "the old games, dances, and songs are fast becoming extinct, and the Passamaquoddy has lost almost everything which characterized his fathers."

Edison promoted his phonograph as a machine for office dictation, for parlor games, or even for storing the voices of loved ones before they departed. Fewkes, in some ways, had a far larger vision. He saw that he could use the new recording technology to capture the voice of an entire culture even as it was passing away.

The phonograph Fewkes used weighed about a hundred pounds; brown wax covered the cylinders, and a speaking horn funneled the voice down to the diaphragm. The size of the cylinder had increased from four to six inches, giving a total playing time of two to four minutes—still not enough to capture a long chant or story. Recording with this Edison phonograph was truly a hit-or-miss proposition. Was the stylus actually incising the wax cylinder? And how fast should the cylinder be cranked to get an accurate recording? Despite these uncertainties, the beauty of the wax cylinder lay in its reusable nature. A badly recorded cylinder could be recycled by carefully shaving away the incised grooves and starting all over again.

Attentive to "his master's voice," the trademark mutt, Nipper, seems as fascinated by the disc gramophone as the listening public was. Turn-of-the-century artist Francis Barraud first painted his pet listening to an Edison cylinder phonograph. When Edison agents in London showed no interest, Barraud took his painting to representatives of Émile Berliner [OPPOSITE], inventor of the gramophone, and Nipper eventually became the symbol for Berliner's American company, Victor, as well as for his two European concerns—Deutsche Gramophone and British Gramophone, later EMI.

Armed with a foot-treadle-powered phonograph, Fewkes arrived in pueblo country. He was "particularly anxious to record the songs connected with the celebration of the midsummer dances, which occur at or near the summer solstice." He accomplished that and spent four years studying Zuni society and archaeological ruins in the area. But for unknown reasons, he apparently made no recordings after 1891.

Though the talking machine had made members of a Washington scientific audience faint, the Zuni, Fewkes reported, "are not afraid of it, and there is no difficulty in getting them to talk into the instrument. The great difficulty in getting them to repeat their sacred songs and prayers does not come so much from their fear of the instrument as of secularizing what is sacred to them."

Maybe Fewkes pushed a little too hard on this front, because one Hopi reported that, when Fewkes returned to study the Hopi for the Bureau of Ethnology in 1898, he was apparently visited one night by the fearsome earth god, Masauwu, who threatened him until he agreed to adopt Hopi beliefs—and presumably stop his confounded note taking. Fewkes left Walpi pueblo soon thereafter. The official explanation for his hasty departure was to avoid a local outbreak of smallpox.

LIKE THE PUEBLO INDIANS, MANY NATIVE CULTURES understood the spiritual power of music. By the late 19TH century, music had become the key to survival for the Plains Indians. Even as Fewkes began his recordings, the American Plains were being swept by a messianic movement called the Ghost Dance. Wearing "ghost shirts" empowered with the symbols of eagles and bison, dancers began their ritual, sure that the shirts would protect them from the bullets of white men. The performers believed that if they kept dancing, they could raise their dead—humans and bison—and that the accursed white man would disappear from the face of the Earth.

On a frigid December morning in 1890, just nine months after Fewkes
had recorded the Passamaquoddy in Maine, U.S. troops tried to stop a
Sioux Ghost Dance being held at Wounded Knee in South Dakota.
When the Indians resisted, the troops slaughtered 150 men, women,
and children and left their bodies to freeze in the snow. It took three
days before "a long trench was dug and into it were thrown all the
bodies, piled one upon another like so much cordwood…," observer
James Mooney wrote, adding, "Whites…went out in order to get the
'ghost shirts,' and the frozen bodies were thrown into the trench
stiff and naked."

Mooney, an anthropologist with the Bureau of Ethnology, understood
the significance of the Ghost Dance and had gone out to the Plains to
study the songs and beliefs associated with it. He saw the dance as a
spiritual revival that occurs "but once in the life of a race." Even after

Wounded Knee, the Ghost Dance persisted, and Mooney kept studying it. Like Fewkes, he began using the phonograph to record Plains songs, believing that the music mirrored the Indians' mythology and spiritual beliefs—and that all the pieces of the Indian world could be wiped out as easily as had been the Sioux at Wounded Knee.

> "I can still see the butchered women and children lying heaped and scattered all along the crooked gulch....And I can see that something else died there in the bloody mud, and was buried in the blizzard. A people's dream died there. It was a beautiful dream...." —Black Elk, *Sioux visionary*

Even as the Indians struggled to survive, the Victorian world put on vast and fantastical shows—world's fairs—to celebrate human accomplishments across continents and cultures. In 1893, in the very heart of what had been the Plains Indians' world and was now the city of Chicago, the World's Columbian Exposition was held to celebrate the 400TH anniversary of Columbus's "discovery" of the New World. Showcasing Indians as cultural specimens, anthropologists arranged dioramas and other exhibits to highlight their work in studying various Native American tribes. The fair also celebrated many other cultures—

and the wonders of the phonograph. Under the sponsorship of the ever generous Mary Hemenway, Harvard psychologist Benjamin Ives Gilman took the opportunity to do a little fieldwork at the fair. He made 101 wax cylinder recordings of music from the fair's different cultures, from Javanese gamelan music to Turkish vocal and instrumental music to the ceremonial songs of the Kwakiutl of Vancouver Island.

Before his fieldwork at the fair, Gilman had been busy transcribing some of Fewkes's pueblo cylinders, and he clearly recognized their value. "A collection by phonographic cylinders like that obtained by Dr. Fewkes forms a permanent museum of primitive music...." In his analysis of the Fewkes material, Gilman himself blazed new trails. He understood that this music was not structured like Western music, and he therefore published the Zuni and Hopi transcriptions without any key or time signatures. When he worked with the cylinders, he carefully recorded the rotation speed of the machine and other details that would affect the sound.

Not so his direct competitor in this new work of transcription— musician John Comfort Fillmore. Fillmore "refined" the transcriptions of Omaha music collected by ethnologist Alice Cunningham Fletcher. "The music did not 'sound natural' to them," she explained to Fillmore of the solos she transcribed, then played back on the piano to her informants. "But when I added a simple harmony my ear was content and the Indians were satisfied." With Fletcher's blessing, Fillmore added chords and harmonies to the transcriptions, even though the Indians actually sang in unison. "I am profoundly convinced that the Indian always intends to sing precisely the same harmonic intervals which are the staple of our own music, and that all aberrations from harmonic pitch are mere accidents due...to imperfect training, or rather to the total lack of it," he wrote. Fillmore went even further with the music. Inspired by the nationalist trend in music emanating from Europe, he used the Omaha sounds as he composed what he considered truly American works with such names as "Indian Fantasia Number One for Full Orchestra." Despite Fillmore's ethnocentric approach and the prevailing attitudes of the times, the cylinders eventually would come to stand as treasures in their own right, as Gilman had predicted. Fletcher herself left behind a wealth of cylinders.

[OPPOSITE] Controversial anthropologist Frank Hamilton Cushing, dressed as a "mud head" for the Zuni mud dance, developed his own controversial fieldwork methods while working among pueblo peoples in the 1880s. By adopting their ways, he hoped to penetrate their world. "I have gained a position among the shaman that I never hoped to get," he wrote in one letter. "Now they urge information and opportunities on me—nothing is withheld."

> **1890**

A coin-operated cylinder phonograph with listening tubes ushers in the age of the juke box.

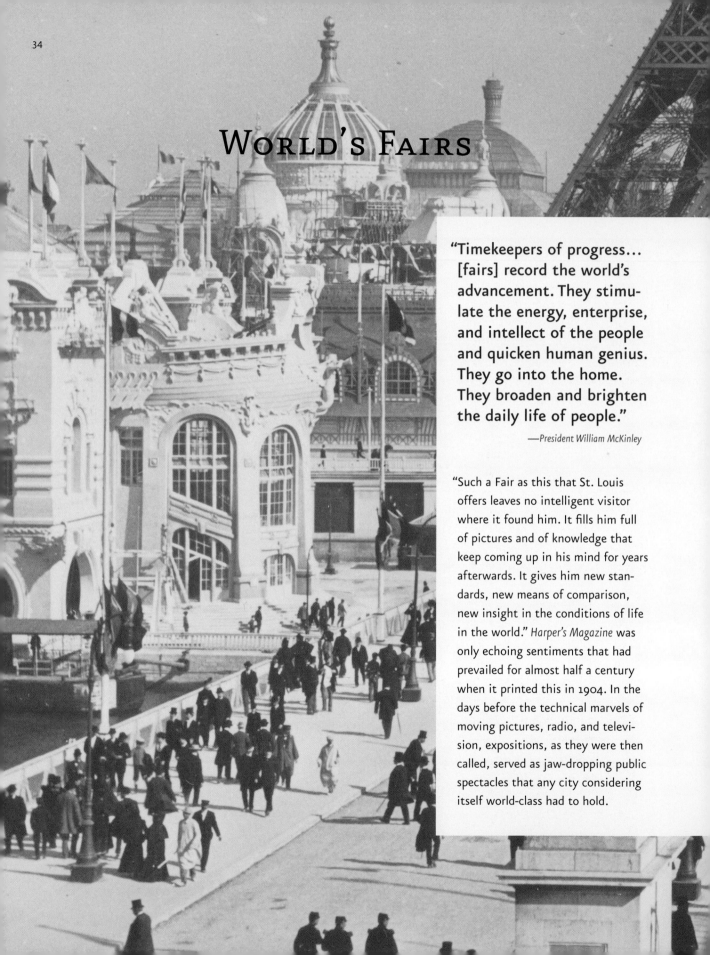

WORLD'S FAIRS

"Timekeepers of progress... [fairs] record the world's advancement. They stimulate the energy, enterprise, and intellect of the people and quicken human genius. They go into the home. They broaden and brighten the daily life of people."

—*President William McKinley*

"Such a Fair as this that St. Louis offers leaves no intelligent visitor where it found him. It fills him full of pictures and of knowledge that keep coming up in his mind for years afterwards. It gives him new standards, new means of comparison, new insight in the conditions of life in the world." *Harper's Magazine* was only echoing sentiments that had prevailed for almost half a century when it printed this in 1904. In the days before the technical marvels of moving pictures, radio, and television, expositions, as they were then called, served as jaw-dropping public spectacles that any city considering itself world-class had to hold.

The beginning of these Victorian extravaganzas is usually traced to the 1851 Crystal Palace Exposition in London's Hyde Park—also called the Great Exposition of the Works of Industry of All Nations. William Makepeace Thackeray parodied its grandeur and effect in verse—and gave the world a new term: "With conscious proide / I stood insoide / And looked the World's Great Fair in. / Until me sight / Was dazzled quite,/ And couldn't see for staring." Pride, industry, dazzling sights—all these elements came to characterize the great 19th-century "world's fairs." They were markets where the newest industrial and technological wonders could be shown off to potential buyers; they were trade shows and scholarly gatherings; they were entertainment centers, where hoochee-koochee dancers performed; they were the "world's universities"; and they were, at their core, successful business ventures and emblems of national success and patriotic pride.

The Crystal Palace attracted over six million visitors in its five-and-a-half-month run. It was followed four years later by a Paris exposition. Thereafter, London and Paris took turns holding a quick succession of fairs, with Vienna holding one as well in 1873. New York, too, tried its hand, with its own 1853 Crystal Palace Exposition, but the fair was a financial failure. It would take Americans 23 years before they had another go at it, and this time they were successful. The 1876 Centennial International Exhibition—honoring the birth of the nation—was held in Philadelphia. Whereas a single building had been constructed for the misbegotten New York fair, this exposition filled Fairmont Park with five major structures—with names like the Horticultural Building and the Machinery Building—and 26 smaller ones, all connected by avenues and greenswards.

11725—Trocadero Entrance to the Exposition, Colonial Section in Foreground, Paris, 1900.

The exposition's centerpiece, the Main Exhibition Building, measured 1,880 feet long and 464 feet wide and was the largest in the world. The public responded enthusiastically to such extravagance, and ten million people eventually strolled through the fairgrounds.

By 1893, America was ready for another international exposition, and Chicago, New York, and St. Louis vied with each other for the privilege and profits accrued in holding it. Chicago took the prize and began planning the World's Columbian Exposition, to commemorate Columbus's arrival in America 400 years earlier. Even more ambitious than Philadelphia's fair, Chicago's White City, as it came to be called, sprawled on the marshy shores of Lake Michigan. Fair planners hired the firm of Burnham and Root as architects, and Daniel Burnham steamed forward under his own credo: "Make no little plans."

Ethnologists and anthropologists figured prominently in the planning of this fair, and they were anxious to use it as an opportunity to familiarize the public with their work. A few years earlier, yet another Paris exposition had featured a "colonial city," with ethnological displays from various cultures, and the Chicago fair followed suit. The respected Harvard ethnologist Frederic Ward Putnam and his assistant Franz Boas took over much of the planning. Along the mile-long Midway Plaisance, Japanese and Javanese, Samoans and Algerians, Apaches and Navajos became part of living exhibits that featured the architecture, art, music, and industry of their different cultures. But the Midway also had concessions and honky-tonk entertainers and the popular 264-foot-high wheel designed by George Ferris.

As the century turned, America sought to court its southern neighbors and to that end staged the Pan American Exposition in Buffalo, New York. Though the fair was not particularly notable in and of itself, it did change the course of history as no other exposition ever had. When President William McKinley—an ardent fairgoer—made an official visit, he was shot twice by an anarchist and died eight days later of his wounds. Vice President Theodore Roosevelt succeeded him and changed the course of the nation.

A few more great American fairs would follow, notably the St. Louis fair of 1904, whose sprawling grounds were almost twice that of Chicago's. They would all leave their mark on the minds of the fairgoers and on the landscapes of cities. Philadelphia still boasts the decaying grandeur of a few fair buildings, as does St. Louis. And Chicago's Field Museum is a direct offspring of that city's fair. But as one Chicago fairgoer predicted. "The people who could dream this vision and make it real ... would press on to greater victories than this triumph of beauty— victories greater than the world had yet witnessed." He was right. Those victories have come, and their coming has signaled the passing of the great expositions.

[PRECEDING PAGES] The 1889 Universal Exposition in Paris stretched below its showcase feature, the 1,051-foot Eiffel Tower, highest and most innovative structure of its time. The fair's "colonial city," where Asian and African participants occupied simulated native villages, inspired planners of the 1893 World's Columbian Exposition in Chicago to attempt a similar series of displays, featuring foreign and Native American cultures [ABOVE].

A Javanese gamelan orchestra and masked dancers brought the music of their island to Americans attending the 1893 World's Columbian Exposition. Ethnologists and songcatchers, too, converged on the fair, to share research and ideas.

[OPPOSITE] Alice Fletcher presented three papers on Plains Indians music, and, though she found the scholarly reception to her work deeply disappointing at the time, she ultimately became a legendary anthropologist and songcatcher.

A DECADE BEFORE JESSE FEWKES ever ventured into the field, Alice Fletcher had begun working with the Omaha. As a well-heeled woman in her 40s, she had been, among other things, the administrator for the Women's Indian Association, an organization that made small loans to Indian peoples. In 1880 she met Francis and Susette La Flesche, the adult children of Omaha chief Joseph La Flesche. The La Flesche siblings were in Boston raising public awareness of the plight of their kinsmen the Poncas, Nebraska Indians who were being forcibly removed to Indian Territory. The year after meeting them, Fletcher was headed to the Omaha reservation herself, intent on studying Indians on their home ground—and probably on bringing a touch of adventure to her staid life. Before going, she was warned by Thomas Henry Tibbles, an Indian rights advocate and fiancé of Susette La Flesche: "You'll have to sleep on the cold ground. The food will be strange to you. You'll meet storms on the open prairie and will be wet to the skin.... You'll have no privacy night and day. I'm sure you can never endure it."

Tibbles was wrong. Fletcher would spend the next three decades studying the cultures and languages of the Plains Indians, lobbying for them in Washington—and recording their music.

After a life spent among the proper society of the Northeast, Fletcher seems to have come into her own living among the Omaha on the Plains: "I would like to give you a day of this free life," she wrote to a friend back East. "I like it. I like to feel the wind blow, and to be with these simple folk, who believe what is said, and are not full of all sorts of notions, at least of notions that are a trouble to such as we are."

Fletcher's work was often a cooperative effort between herself and Francis La Flesche, the young Omaha she had first met in the East.

"I heard little or nothing of Indian music the first three or four times that I attended dances or festivals, beyond a screaming downward movement that was gashed and torn by the vehemently beaten drum...," she confessed. "I therefore began to listen below this noise, much as one must listen to the phonograph, ignoring the sound of the machinery...." —*Alice Fletcher*

A man straddling two cultures, La Flesche had grown up on the Nebraska prairie in a settlement other Indians referred to derisively as the village of "Make Believe White Men." His father, Iron Eyes (Joseph), was the last head chief of the Omaha, despite the fact that he was half French. The young La Flesche had been educated in the ways of the whites at a Presbyterian missionary school, but he'd also grown up observing the rituals of his people. His education and sensitivity to both white and Indian ways made him an effective advocate for Indian rights and invaluable to Fletcher. In 1891, she legally adopted him. In the course of his life, he would move to Fletcher's Capitol Hill house in Washington, travel in intellectual circles there, and become a respected anthropologist and songcatcher in his own right.

It was probably La Flesche who first used the phonograph to record Omaha music in 1895. Like other anthropologists of their era, Fletcher and La Flesche saw the cylinders themselves simply as tools from which written transcriptions could be made, analyzed, and studied. To them, the recordings had no worth on their own. As she studied them, though, Fletcher came to understand the music and the way vocables—the sound syllables often used in Native American

> 1895

In Italy, Guglielmo Marconi makes breakthroughs in wireless telegraphy that will revolutionize communications.

singing—were meant to express emotions. To the Indians, she observed, Western singing seemed to have a great deal of talk in it.

Fletcher never felt that she achieved the professional respect she was due from the Bureau of American Ethnology, which had hired her as a "collaborator," nor from her anthropological colleagues.

"Living with my Indian friends I found I was a stranger in my native land.... I learned to hear the echoes of a time when every living thing, even the sky, had a voice. That voice devoutly heard by the ancient people of America I desired to make audible to others."

[OPPOSITE] Morning chores occupy Alice Fletcher (at the washboard), her assistant Jane Gay, and helper James Stuart at their simple cabin on the Nez Perce reservation. Fletcher and her collaborator Francis La Flesche [BELOW], an Omaha Indian, made hundreds of field recordings of Omaha and other Plains Indians music. An early advocate of Indian rights, Fletcher championed the ill-fated allotment system of the 1880s, which divided tribally held land into individually owned parcels.

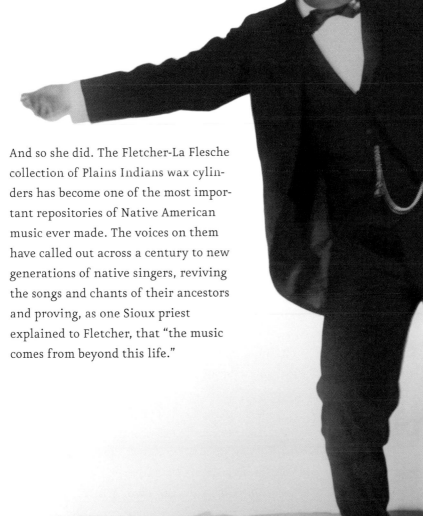

And so she did. The Fletcher-La Flesche collection of Plains Indians wax cylinders has become one of the most important repositories of Native American music ever made. The voices on them have called out across a century to new generations of native singers, reviving the songs and chants of their ancestors and proving, as one Sioux priest explained to Fletcher, that "the music comes from beyond this life."

The 1916 image of Frances Densmore and Blackfoot leader Mountain Chief listening to a cylinder recording has become a symbol of the early songcatcher era. During half a century, Densmore field recorded voraciously, often making transcriptions [OPPOSITE] of the recordings.

FLETCHER'S WRITING AND WORK INFLUENCED the growing number of field recordists and inspired another woman to take to the field. Unlike Fletcher, Frances Densmore was a child of the Plains, born in Red Wing, Minnesota, and educated as a musician at Oberlin College, in Ohio. In 1903 she made her first foray into songcatching, taking notes on the songs of a Sioux, Good Bear Woman, near Red Wing. A year later she traveled a bit farther afield. "Many have written concerning various phases of Philipino life and character but I claim for myself the honor of being the first professional musician to seriously study their music…I remained three weeks, going from one village to another, day after day….Not for any money would I have parted with the sensation of having been the only white woman in a village filled with the most ferocious savages in the world."

The village Densmore visited was actually located within the 1904 St. Louis World's Fair. There she also recorded Geronimo. The great Apache warrior was on display as if he were a curiosity, making arrowheads and autographing tinted cards of himself. When Densmore asked to hear him sing, "There was a flash in the old eyes behind the steel-rimmed spectacles, a slight drawing up of the aged figure and I confess to a feeling of relief when the crowd swallowed me up." Undeterred, Densmore bided her time, and when the old man began humming while fashioning an arrowhead, she surreptitiously (and by modern standards, unethically) noted down the tune.

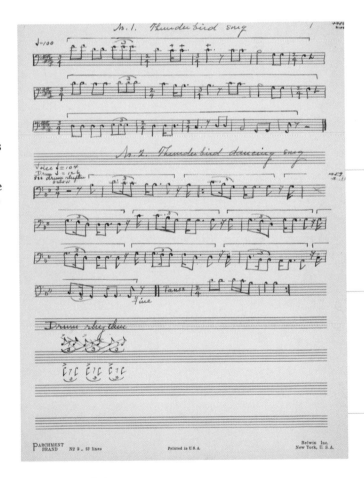

Frances Densmore would spend the next 50 years tirelessly recording American Indian music, but her attitude toward the people she recorded never markedly improved. It was strictly their music she was after. With phonograph in tow, she moved quickly through her fieldwork, usually dominating her informants. "The singer must never be allowed to think that he is in charge of the work," she wrote in the 1940s to an aspiring collector. "Singers should be checked by general reputation. Loud voices are not essential, and men who sing at dances are apt to be too free-and-easy."

The phonograph may have contributed to Densmore's insensitivity. Without it, she would have been forced to spend more time in the field, perhaps learning more about the cultures of Indians she was recording. On the other hand, her speed was probably a blessing to those she recorded. Once, when she had stayed longer in a Ute village than she had originally announced, a resident confronted her. "Why aren't you gone…. You are still here. We don't like it."

Densmore's approach didn't sit well with other anthropologists, either. Though the BAE named her a collaborator, as Fletcher had been, it never quite took her seriously. Neither did the press. A *Time* magazine article called her a "whoop collector," a statement as much a reflection of the times as of Densmore, who, despite her methods, had come to appreciate Indian music as a deep form of expression.

"Music to them, in its highest sense, is connected with power and with communication with the mysterious forces that control all human life. In that, even more than in the sound of the singing, lies the real difference between the music of the American Indian and that of our own race." —*Frances Densmore*

[OPPOSITE] Father of American anthropology, Franz Boas poses here as a Hamatsa, a powerful supernatural figure in Kwakiutl myth. Boas did much of his own fieldwork among the Kwakiutl and other Northwest Coast peoples, but his greatest contributions were as teacher and theorist at Columbia University and public advocate for anthropology at the American Museum of Natural History in New York.

Densmore kept at her work into her late 80s, traveling all over the United States and British Columbia to record the oldest songs before they were lost forever. She sometimes cajoled singers into recording sessions by saying that the cylinders containing their music would be stored in Washington, D.C., in a building that would never burn down. Her promise may have been a ploy, but she was partly right. Her collection today is housed in the Library of Congress's American Folklife Center, where fire has never threatened it—though technical problems have.

In the 1930s and '40s, Densmore had enough vision to understand that her more than 2,000 cylinder recordings should be preserved and the music reproduced for a larger audience. In a letter to the head of the Library of Congress's music division, she wrote that "if musicians are sufficiently interested…there may emerge a dramatic American music that is not folk music nor a foreign importation." It would take decades for that to happen; in the meantime Densmore's cylinder

collection did get transferred to disks. But the process was flawed by something that would plague musical preservationists into the future: recording speed. Densmore said she recorded her graphophone cylinders at 160 rpm, but with a spring-wound graphophone the speed, she admitted, could vary. Many of her cylinders were transferred to disks at too slow a speed; later those disks were used to make master tapes. It was 50 years before the error was discovered and corrected and the sounds of the music made accurate again.

JOHN WESLEY POWELL DIED IN 1902, and with his death the Bureau of American Ethnology, and Washington, lost its hold on American anthropology. Another figure had been emerging on the stage for a decade, a figure who would revolutionize the field, creating a very American brand of anthropology.

Prussian-born Franz Boas was educated as a geographer and physicist in Germany. In 1883, at the age of 25, he went to Baffin Island as an Arctic explorer and mapper, but once there he became captivated by the culture of the Eskimos. "I am now a true Eskimo. I live as they do, hunt with them…" he wrote in a letter.

Franz Boas used his reputation to organize and secure funding for major anthropological field work, notably the far-ranging Jesup Expedition, which lasted years and sent ethnographic research parties throughout the Pacific Northwest and along the Siberian coast.

often had only a few months for fieldwork, and the informant. Without it, the informant would have to repeat and repeat and repeat the same song, chant, story, while the researcher tediously transcribed. While the phonograph did not replace skilled listening and transcribing, it did assist them. But the machine also had limitations. It became an object separating the anthropologist and the informant, putting distance between the two. Then, of course, cylinders could be damaged, lost, or played at the wrong speed, as Densmore's had been. And there were sounds—rattles, drums, high-pitched voices—that did not move enough air to record on wax cylinders. Even though the sounds were intrinsic to the music, they were lost to the limitations of acoustic recording. But the music that the phonograph did manage to record became invaluable.

At the time, the idea of "sound blindness" was in vogue: the notion that some individuals couldn't distinguish differences in key and timbre. Usually, non-Western hearers were diagnosed with this, but the ethnographer could be just as sound blind to the phonemes or musics of other cultures. Boas understood that unfamiliar sounds, both in music and language, might not be easily perceived. "The vibrations of the air...sets in motion the membrane of the tympanum of the hearer, who then perceives the sound. But how does he apperceive it? Only by means of similar sounds he has heard before." The phonograph did not have preconceptions about the sounds it "heard." As long as they were strong enough to move the diaphragm, activate the stylus, and inscribe the wax, they would be recorded.

By the turn of the 20TH century, phonographs all over the world had begun to listen.

3 / unsung heroes

As the 19TH century gave way to the 20TH, America was poised to assume a larger role, culturally and politically, on the world stage—a stage dominated in the West by Europe. The European powers, riding the rising tide of national imperialism, intended to keep it that way.

In 1884, Franz Boas, still in his native Prussia, had written that "one hears nothing but the splendor of the German Empire and the advancement of national interests." Pursuing those national interests, Germany expanded its colonial power, declaring New Guinea and part of Africa German protectorates. As the century came to an end, nationalism had spread across Europe, and had begun to leave its mark on music.

The new politics encouraged a growing European interest in exotic and indigenous folk musics. Since the 16TH-century age of discovery, European intellectuals had been curious about their global neighbors. In the 1700s, European missionaries Jean-Baptiste du Halde and Joseph Amiot made groundbreaking studies of Chinese music. In other corners of the world, missionaries, civil servants, and adventurers were transcribing Arab musics, Indian musics, and Japanese musics, among others. In 1768, Jean-Jacques Rousseau included some of these in his *Dictionnaire de musique*.

Rousseau discussed exotic musics in words and musical notation, though he could not, of course, re-create their sounds. But by the turn of the 20TH century, collectors had two powerful new tools. One was the "cents" system. Developed in the 1880s by English physicist and

> **1898**

Danish inventor Vlademar Poulsen patents technique for making magnetic recording on steel wire.

phonetician Alexander J. Ellis, it divided the octave into 1,200 equal units so that accurate measurements could be made of scales and intervals, thus avoiding any Western assumptions about the universality of pitches, scales, and tuning systems. The other tool was, of course, the phonograph.

The breakthrough work with the phonograph would come in Berlin, where psychologist and philosopher Carl Stumpf hoped to use music to explore the structure of the human brain. To do that, he decided to go beyond only Western music and to begin exploring the music-making of other cultures.

In September 1900, when a visiting Siamese (now Thai) theatre troupe performed in Berlin, Stumpf—then head of the Psychological Institute he had founded at Berlin University—and his colleague Otto Abraham took a phonograph and recorded the Siamese musicians. Having

The phonograph was still a technological marvel when the Siamese Court Orchestra visited Berlin and was recorded by Professor Carl Stumpf. The recording laid the groundwork for the renowned Berlin Phonogramm-Archiv of the world's musics.

analyzed written Siamese music, Stumpf suspected that the Siamese octave had seven steps of equal size, unlike the Western major and minor scales, with seven steps of unequal size. To a European like Stumpf, the Siamese scale went against natural law and seemed therefore to have profound psychological implications. But Stumpf's recording foray would have results that ranged far beyond his own theories. The 24 wax cylinders Stumpf and Abraham made that day signaled the beginning of the most important collection of the world's music ever made: the Berlin Phonogramm-Archiv.

"Without the help of the phonograph, we are left standing in front of museum display cabinets in which instruments are stored in the dumb stillness of the grave, full of wonder and empty of understanding."

—*Artur Simon, Director, Berlin Phonogramm-Archiv*

By 1905, the Phonogramm-Archiv had grown to 10,000 recordings, most on wax cylinders. Since non-Western performers were considered a fashionable entertainment at the time, a steady stream of them came through Berlin, and most were duly recorded, including musicians from India, Japan, and many other countries. Field recordings, too, were now flowing into the archive, the first one made in 1902 in Turkey by an ethnographer, others from East Africa by a linguist. Most were recorded in German colonies in Oceania and Africa; Franz Boas, a friend of Stumpf, sent along his own recordings of Northwest Coast tribes. "In the early years it was a question less of musicologists than ethnologists, linguists, members of expeditions, doctors, missionaries, and interested colonial officials making recordings of traditional music in faraway places for the Berlin Phonogramm-Archiv," explains Artur Simon, Director of the Phonogramm-Archiv since 1972.

The driving force behind the archive in its early years was Erich Von Hornbostel, a well-to-do young Viennese who joined the project as a volunteer and soon rose to be its head. His personal funds fueled the archive for its first three decades, when it received little official

financial backing. Despite the lack of funds, the archive's reputation grew. From the far-flung corners of the world Hornbostel received enthusiastic, or imploring, letters, including one from the noted humanitarian Dr. Albert Schweitzer in Cap Lopez, Africa.

> "Once upon a time a great culture, of its kind, must have held sway here....It is time to record this music. In twenty years time it will no longer exist. Firstly because the young people learn Christian songs from the Mission...[and] In the foreseeable future there will no longer be any daylong journeys by rowing boat, where twenty men in a canoe stand one behind the other and sing, because otherwise they would not be able to keep in time with the rhythm of the rowing."
>
> —*Dr. Albert Schweitzer*

Hornbostel planned to honor Schweitzer's request, but the First World War intervened. When the war was over, a defeated Germany was divested of its colonies, and the flow of music into the archive slowed dramatically. In the economic depression that followed, Hornbostel lost his fortune—and with it the ability to support the archive. In 1922, the Prussian State officially took control of the Berlin Phonogramm-Archiv and stipulated that it generate the funds to support itself. In the years afterward, the archive produced a Demonstration Collection of 120 songs, which took the world's musical treasures from the depths of the archives and presented them to a public audience. The collection would become an enduring symbol of the range of music preserved by the Berlin Phonogramm-Archiv.

[ABOVE] At Camp Frankfurt in 1916, Stumpf (right) and a colleague record Tatar prisoners of war. During the First World War, Stumpf was appointed to the Phonograph Commission. Formed to make linguistic and musical recordings of prisoners, it amassed 1,020 wax cylinders and 1,650 disk recordings.

[OPPOSITE] The label from cylinder # 1 signals the beginning of the Berlin Phonogramm-Archiv. By comparing different musics, the archive's early scholars hoped to identify a progression from simple to complex musics—an evolution that has been long since discredited.

[BELOW] Surrounded by the members of a string quartet, Hungarian composers Béla Bartók (seated left) and Zoltán Kodály (seated right) pose for a 1910 photograph. Both composers were dedicated to uncovering and preserving the folk musics of Central Europe and incorporating traditional themes into their own compositions.

[OPPOSITE] A Palestinian woman sings for posterity as she makes a recording for the Berlin Phonogramm-Archiv.

By 1933 Hornbostel, a Jew, had fled the rising tide of National Socialism in Germany for the U.S. His protégé, Hungarian-born George Herzog, also a Jew, left as well and joined Franz Boas at Columbia University. Boas's reputation—and with it Columbia's—for progressive scholarship had grown well beyond America's boundaries. Herzog was attracted to Boas's inclusive approach to American Indian studies—focusing equally on language, folklore and mythology, art, music, and material culture. He became an exemplar of the high standards Boas set for rigorous field collecting and laboratory analysis. The anthropological approach to the study of musics that Herzog engineered would influence American songcatchers for decades to come.

By the time the Second World War, which had flung so many intellectuals onto American shores, finally ignited in Germany itself, the Berlin Phonogramm-Archiv had grown to some 15,000 recordings. But with the war, the collection was split up, some of the recordings lost, and a large portion taken by the Soviets to Leningrad. Miraculously, roughly 90 per cent of the collection went on to East Berlin and finally back to Berlin with the reunification of Germany in 1991. In September 2000, the Phonogramm-Archiv staged a 100TH anniversary celebration, at which Stumpf's cylinder #1, of the Siamese music, was played. It was followed

by a live performance of the same piece, in its entirety, by a contemporary Thai ensemble. The cylinder's shortened version of the piece was only a shadow-skeleton of the way the music lived among the Thai musicians.

WHEN STUMPF MADE that first cylinder, a handful of European countries dominated Western art music, but change was in the air. The nationalist fervor that swept European politics in the late 19th century had a strong impact on musicians and long-cherished musical traditions. Suddenly, the Austrian Habsburgs, who had dominated the European scene for centuries, began to lose their stranglehold. When Italy and Germany became nation-states, composers such as Giuseppe Verdi and Richard Wagner rose to prominence in the art music of Europe, their works throbbing with a sense of the national soul. But the composers who followed them took nationalism a step further, searching out the folk sounds unique to their countries and using them in their own compositions. The novel harmonies of "peasants" enriched the vocabulary of European art music. In Russia, Glinka, Borodin, and Mussorgsky shaped their compositions with undercurrents of folk song and dance harmonies, melodies, and rhythms. In Czechoslovakia, it was Smetana and Dvorák, in Scandinavia Grieg and Sibelius, in Spain Isaac Albeniz, and in England, Edward Elgar. In Hungary musicians Zoltán Kodály and Béla Bartók did more than just incorporate folk music into their compositions; they searched it out at its source, and Bartók particularly became an obsessive field recordist.

"Allow me to introduce myself. I am a Professor at the Royal Hungarian Academy of Music in Budapest and, in my spare time, undertake a great deal of study of folk music, to be precise as a collector," Bartók wrote to Erich Von Hornbostel at the Berlin Phonogramm-Archiv in May 1912. By then he had been collecting seriously for ten years, at the same time pursuing a career as a concert pianist and

> 1919

Radio Corporation of America is formed from American Marconi Company, appropriated by the U.S. from the British Marconi Company in WWI.

[RIGHT] Béla Bartók gathers musical residents of a Slovak village around his phonograph on a collecting foray into the countryside. "The Edison phonograph invented folk music recording," Bartók proclaimed, and he continued to record on portable, lightweight wax-cylinder phonographs well after newer technologies were available.

[BOTTOM] In 1936, Bartók (middle) traveled through parts of Turkey with his colleague Adnan Saygun and made numerous cylinder recordings of the music of its peoples, among them the nomadic Kumarli [OPPOSITE].

> 1920s

Age of electrical recording, using microphones and amplification, begins.

composer. Born in 1881 in an area that later became part of Romania, Bartók lived in a corner of central Europe influenced by a mix of cultures—Hungarian, Romanian, German, and others. In 1905, after graduating from the Academy of Music, he met Kodály, who had already begun studying Hungarian folk music. Bartók himself quickly took up the pursuit: "I have a new plan now, to collect the finest examples of Hungarian folk-songs, and to raise them to the level of works of art with the best possible piano accompaniment."

Bartók realized that what had been called Hungarian folk music in the past was no more than what he called "gypsy slop." A man of his time, Bartók used the phrase as an all-purpose condemnation of anything inauthentic, unoriginal, or hybridized. Along with the other musical nationalists, Bartók was searching for purity in music. In 1906 and 1907, he set out on his first collecting forays into the Hungarian countryside, leaving behind the comforts of city life. Like most collectors, he was faced with the discomforts of primitive conditions and reluctant folk musicians who had to be cajoled with patience and tact. But what he found made the hardships worthwhile. In Transylvania, he believed he had discovered an ancient form of Hungarian music based on the pentatonic scale. It was a long way from the popular gypsy music heard in the cafés of Budapest, but it was only the beginning for Bartók. In the following decades, he would continue to scour the central European countryside, his collecting forays taking him to Turkey and Algeria. Though he was recording on Edison wax cylinders, his real goal, as with all collectors of that era, was to transcribe the music onto paper. His son, Peter, remembered that "many a night I went to sleep while the ground glass door separating my bedroom from my father's study showed his table lamp on, until the small hours of the night, and I heard the odd sounds of his cylinder record machine playing fragments of a song, bagpipe music, or the like, at some very slow speed, little bits at a time over and over."

"I have seen no jeweller handling precious stones or gold objects with the kind of gentle care as my father held one of those cylinders in his hands, touching on the outer edges, placing them on the machine gently; wrapping each one afterwards in silky, soft paper as a protection against scratching and mold....These cylinders contained recorded music no-one could duplicate today, regardless of the sophisticated technology...." —Peter Bartók

ARCHIVING SOUND

Though recording technology was first developed in the United States, archiving recorded sound was initially a European idea. In 1899 a Viennese physiologist founded the Phonogramm-Archiv of the Akademie der Wissenschaften, and a year later in Germany the Berlin Phonogramm-Archiv was established.

[Opposite] Songcatcher Percy Grainger works with a staff member at the Library of Congress to preserve his folksong collection.

[Below] During World War II, the American Broadcasting Station in Europe operated as a temporary archive of sound and music.

Both institutions gathered recordings of non-Western musics that were of interest to researchers in music, acoustics, and psychology, thus making possible comparative and cross-cultural studies of the world's musics.

In the first half of the 20TH century, other important European sound archives were established in major cities: In Paris, the Archive de la Parole (1911) and later the Phonothèque Nationale (1938); the Discoteca di Stato (1928) in Rome; the Glinka Museum of Musical Culture (1937) in Moscow; and in London, the British Institute of Recorded Sound (1948). Radio stations also played a significant role in sound archiving, sometimes retaining their instantaneous recordings of programs, sometimes placing those recordings in other archives. Early programs from the British Broadcasting Corporation, founded in 1922, are now part of the British Library Sound Archives.

In the United States, the Library of Congress announced a plan to estab-

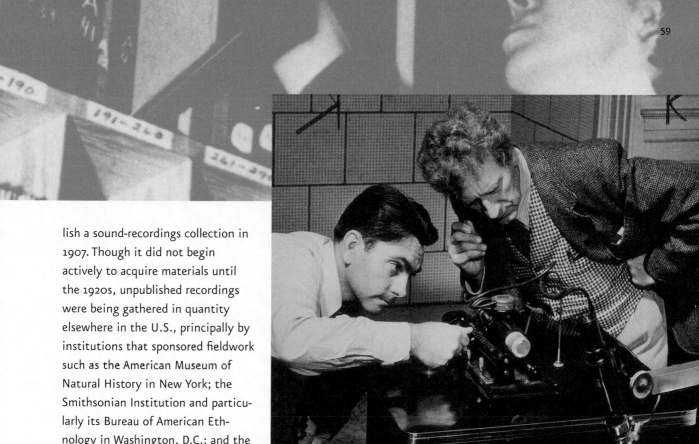

lish a sound-recordings collection in 1907. Though it did not begin actively to acquire materials until the 1920s, unpublished recordings were being gathered in quantity elsewhere in the U.S., principally by institutions that sponsored fieldwork such as the American Museum of Natural History in New York; the Smithsonian Institution and particularly its Bureau of American Ethnology in Washington, D.C.; and the School of American Research in Santa Fe. University-based museums, especially Harvard's Peabody Museum and U.C. Berkeley's Phoebe A. Hearst Museum, served as early repositories of faculty-student collections.

In many cases, the early recordings were made by anthropologists and linguists who were aware of the importance of music as a form of cultural expression but who felt themselves incapable of analyzing the music itself. Since they could make phonetic transcriptions of spoken words, and therefore oral traditions, for their own future research, they did not record these, focusing instead on recording music. But the musical

recordings they made often were passed on to their institutions, remaining untouched for years.

The names of two European-born anthropologists appear frequently in the history of American ethnographic recordings: Franz Boas (1858-1942) and George Herzog (1901-1983) both conducted research themselves and made sound recordings, and each in turn taught the next generation of anthropologists and ethnomusicologists. Boas, who was at Columbia University in New York from 1899 until 1936, taught Herzog, Alfred Kroeber (who went to

Berkeley and with his students created extensive documentation of California native communities), and Helen Roberts (known particularly for her recordings of native Californians). Boas also organized the turn-of-the-century Jesup North Pacific Expedition for the American Museum of Natural History, and the expedition's participants made extensive ethnographic field recordings.

George Herzog and Helen Roberts worked together in the first part of the 1930s at the interdisciplinary Yale Institute of Human Relations, in New Haven, Connecticut.

In the latter half of the 20TH century, ethnographic collections were in many cases consolidated, particularly as early sound-recording formats became obsolete and only a few places had recording engineers and equipment able to handle them. Thus, sound collections from institutions like the Peabody Museum, the Wheelwright Museum, the Milwaukee Public Museum, the Southwest Museum, the State Historical Society of North Dakota, as well as the Bureau of American Ethnology and Columbia University, were loaned to the Archive of Folk Culture for copying or transferred there entirely. Now, historic recordings by Boas, Herzog, Roberts, and others are housed at the Library of Congress.

Among other activities, they preserved original cylinder recordings, obtained from various researchers and museums, by copying them onto aluminum discs. When Herzog returned to Columbia, some of the Yale cylinders were transferred to the Archives of Folk and Primitive Music that Herzog established there, as were field recordings collected for the American Museum of Natural History. In 1948, Herzog moved to Indiana University, and the entire Columbia archive moved with him, forming the basis for the renowned Archives of Traditional Music.

Ironically, the sound archive that would eventually became the largest such repository in the country had few connections to Boas, Herzog, or Columbia University. The Archive of American Folk Song (now the Archive of Folk Culture) in the Library of Congress was the brainchild of Robert Winslow Gordon (1888-1961), who, after studying literature at Harvard and teaching at Berkeley, had set off in 1925 to record American folk songs. By 1928 he had succeeded in establishing a national folk song archive at the library. Gordon, his immediate successors—John Lomax and his son Alan—and the staff that followed them went on field trips to document American folk song, folklife, and oral traditions, making the archive the only part of the Library that actively creates collections, as well as receiving them from donors.

Though the transfer of recordings from one institution to another over time has often helped preserve the sound, it has exacerbated the documentation process. Written and photographic documentation and related materials were often retained by the collectors themselves or by earlier repositories. And the movement from one location to another created added confusion in cataloguing, as many different numbers could be attached to a single recording—a collector's number, a performer's number, a museum

repository number, an archive cat-
alog number, a location number.
These realities pose challenges to
all researchers and create complex
questions about rights and permis-
sions for the archives in which the
recordings are now housed.

But the greatest challenge comes
in trying to preserve the recording
media themselves before they
deteriorate. In recent years, the Save
Our Sounds project has been started
as a joint endeavor between the
Library of Congress's American Folklife Center and the Smithsonian
Institution's Center for Folklife and
Cultural Heritage. The project mission is "to preserve historical American audio recordings so that they
may educate, inform, and inspire
generations to come." Throughout
the world, audiovisual archives are
actively involved in preservation
efforts to save the sounds—and
sights—that give depth to our
understanding of the past.

JUDITH GRAY
American Folklife Center

[RIGHT] Robert Winslow Gordon, who
founded the Archive of American Folk Song
at the Library of Congress.

[OPPOSITE, TOP] Deteriorating wax cylinders will give up their treasures unless the
sound on them is transferred to a more
permanent medium.

[BELOW] Edvard Grieg (far left) and Percy Grainger (middle) visit at Grieg's Norwegian country home, Troldhaugen, just before the elder composer's death in August 1907. The two shared a love of folk music and wove folk themes into their own compositions.

[OPPOSITE] Grainger (standing) used his considerable talents as both a composer and a performer to promote the folk music he collected.

> **1931**

On Abbey Road in London, EMI opens the largest recording studio in the world.

Bartók's friend and collaborator, Kodály, also wrote admiringly of Bartók's passion for collecting and analyzing the world's music. "He spent one summer near the North Pole, another in Africa. Had he not lived between the two world wars, he would surely have encircled the globe." But he did live then, and in the 1930s, after the German occupation of Austria, he became increasingly worried. "I feel rather uncomfortable to live so very near to the clutches of the Nazis or even in their clutches...." he wrote a friend in January 1939.

In early 1940, Bartók made an exploratory concert tour of the United States with his wife, Ditta Pasztory, also a pianist. When he returned to his beloved Hungary, he packed up and left permanently. To Kodály he turned over his Hungarian folk song collection; he shipped other parts of the collection with his personal belongings to New York. But the British authorities held up the trunks for political reasons, and for a time, it seemed that Bartók's painstakingly collected folk music might be lost in the chaos of war. Eventually, it made its way to America, where the musician and his wife had taken up residence in a modest Manhattan apartment. Like Boas and George Herzog, Bartók landed at Columbia, where he continued to work on his Romanian folk music collection.

With the war's end, Bartók, by then seriously ill with leukemia, received devastating news from Zoltán Kodály. In April 1945, robbers had broken into the Ethnographical Museum in Budapest, destroying cylinders of irretrievable folk music and, with them, as the local papers reported, "the work of 40 years." But Kodály also wrote that

Grainger's energy was legendary, and he brought it all to bear in his collecting. He would greet farmers in fields and ask if they knew any of the old songs they could sing for him. He sought out people in the Brigg workhouse, once even taking the phonograph to record a particularly talented old singer in his hospital bed. Irrepressible, even unethical, Grainger wouldn't give up when stalking music. When a woman whose songs he coveted refused to sing for him, he had her daughter sneak him into the family's home. He hid under the bed, taking notations as the daughter cajoled her mother into singing her a few songs.

Grainger's passion for collecting only increased in the coming years, taking him to other parts of the English countryside; to the largely rural Danish peninsula of Jutland; to remote areas of his native Australia and New Zealand and other parts of the South Seas; even to London, where he recorded the cries of street vendors. All of this he had to accomplish between, or sometimes while on, concert tours. Initially, he seems to have been mostly concerned with preserving the pure forms of folk musics before they disappeared in the wake of "progress." Grainger's own background kept him free of the modes of

[ABOVE] Grainger found the phonograph indispensable to his work as a folk music collector, believing that it captured the nuances and style of an individual performer—subtleties that written transcriptions neglected altogether.

[OPPOSITE] In New Zealand, Grainger was delighted to discover recordings of Rarotongan and Maori musics made by A. J. Knocks (right).

> **1935**

In Berlin, BASF/AEG demonstrate the Magnetophone, a device for recording on magnetic tape.

Anglican Church music that biased the ears of other collectors. He understood that, in transcribing songs, standard musical notations were sadly wanting and didn't reflect the subtleties of the singer's performance. This attitude put him squarely at odds with the practices of the English Folk-Song Society. "In transcribing a song," Cecil Sharp, the guiding force behind the society, wrote him, "our aim should be to record its artistic effect, not necessarily the exact means by which that effect was produced...."

Generally rejected by English collectors, Grainger had little to do with them after about 1909, but his impact would prove more far-reaching than theirs. His arrangements of folk songs became immensely popular and brought the public to a new appreciation of the old melodies. It was Grainger, through an adaptation he made, who popularized an old melody as the perennial favorite *Danny Boy*. Musical royalties, particularly from Grainger's setting of *Country Gardens*, English morris dance melodies initially collected by Cecil Sharp himself, provided Grainger with an income and allowed some of Sharp's own collection to see the light of day.

CECIL SHARP, IN MOST WAYS, WAS GRAINGER'S OPPOSITE.
And yet the reserved Englishman was at the center of the folk song
revival that swept Britain, and to some extent America, early in the
20TH century. Initially a teacher at a boys' school, Sharp wanted to
break out of the tradition of using German music to educate
English children. Gradually, he realized the music of his own
"peasantry" could do that. Like Grainger, he was inspired by the work
of Lucy Broadwood, the folk song collector. But his real inspiration
came one day while sitting in a country garden. Suddenly, he realized
that the gardener was singing to himself as he worked, and that the
song was a genuine folk melody.

> "The folk-song is like the duck-billed platypus in this particular,
> you can live for years within a few yards of it and never suspect
> its existence...." —*Cecil Sharp*

Collecting soon became Sharp's preoccupation, and he spread the good
word about folk music and dance through lectures and classes and
through the Folk-Song Society. Unlike Grainger, he did his collecting
by notation, claiming that recording with the phonograph intimidated
the singer. His collecting forays were sometimes "disturbed by the
noisy entrance of the grandchildren, who would be shocked to find
their grandparents singing their silly old songs to the gentleman, and
would endeavour to reinstate the family reputation by turning on
the gramophone with the latest musical-hall records." Often the old
melodies were being preserved by "Gypsy" (Romani) families in the
English countryside, whose transient lifestyle made them repositories
of music from many regions. Sharp wrote especially enthusiastically of
his meeting with one young Romani family, whom he came upon in a
"peaceful little scene" on the moor. The husband showed Sharp "the
contrivances for making a tent in which they camped out every
night—only using his van during winter." When the young wife came
out, Sharp persuaded her to sing: "She sat down on a stone, gave her
baby the breast, and then began a murder song that was just fasci-
nating. Talk of folk-singing! It was the finest and most characteristic
bit of singing I had ever heard."

In 1914, Sharp sailed for New York to help a friend with the musical
numbers in a Broadway production of *A Midsummer Night's Dream*.
Along with his theater work, he began lecturing and teaching folk
dance—a new rage in America. A year later, he was back in the U.S.

Averse to the phonograph, prominent
English folk song collector Cecil Sharp (left)
transcribed the music he collected from
singers like this Warwickshire man.

In collecting expeditions through Appalachia, Cecil Sharp transcribed the music while his colleague Maud Karpeles took down the words to songs. Owing to the remoteness of the Appalachian villages, Sharp felt the English ballads he discovered in America were less changed by time than the versions sung in England.

to direct a summer school in Maine on the same subjects. Before the school began, Sharp was visited by Olive Dame Campbell. Campbell and her husband, John, had traveled through the southern Appalachians, reporting on the social conditions of the isolated mountain people there. Though John died in 1919, Olive went on to found the progressive John C. Campbell Folk High School to educate mountain people in western North Carolina. (The 2001 Hollywood film *Songcatcher* was probably based on Campbell and on other female ethnomusicologists, such as Dorothy Scarborough, who wrote *Songcatcher in the Southern Appalachians*.)

Campbell was an amateur song collector when she visited Sharp, and she brought him a stack of the musical notations she had made of mountain folk ballads, apologizing for her transcriptions. But Sharp took time to examine the whole pile of transcriptions and declared them "original and valuable material." In fact, the material had convinced him that America's eastern mountains must harbor isolated communities where English folk traditions were preserved in a purer form than he could find in England itself.

Over the course of the next two years, Sharp and his colleague, Maud Karpeles, crisscrossed the deep mountain territory of Tennessee, North Carolina, Virginia, West Virginia, and Kentucky, searching for singers who knew the old tunes. Karpeles had been a folk dance student of Sharp's in England, then became his assistant. As the two

toured the Appalachian backcountry, she took down the words to ballads and Sharp transcribed the music. To allay unwarranted suspicions among the mountain people, Sharp would sometimes introduce her as his adopted daughter.

Usually Sharp and Karpeles went by horse and buggy or wagon, and Sharp, always anxious and often sickly, found the "nerve-strain" of the travel "really awful. How we went over those roads…I cannot tell you. They were at times nothing but a morass, at others a dry creek-bed strewn with boulders." Often, they walked to an isolated cabin, whose inhabitant was said to be a good singer—only to lose their way or find the person unavailable. Still, they kept at it, despite bad food (mostly "hog-meat" or food fried in hog fat), poor accommodations (in the one- or two-room cabins of the mountain people), and frequent illness (on Sharp's part). What gave grace to the hard times was the hospitality of the mountain people and the beauty of the mountains. "I don't ever think I have seen such lovely trees, ferns, and wild flowers...," Sharp wrote.

The songs, he felt, reflected English tunes now lost to his homeland. And he admired the singers.

"Just English peasants in appearance, speech, and manner [they have] an American quality.... They own their own land and have done so for three or four generations, so that there is none of the servility which unhappily is one of the characteristics of the English peasant."

—*Cecil Sharp*

In 1924, Sharp began planning another collecting trip, this time to Canada—"a dive into Newfoundland" to "prospect for songs and ballads." But when Sharp died the same year in England, Maud Karpeles continued with his plans and spent two summers in 1929 and 1930 collecting in Newfoundland on her own—a bold achievement for a woman at that time. The ballads she collected, along with the Appalachian and English folk dance work, earned Karpeles her own respected place among the folk revivalists.

In the course of their mountain rambles, Sharp and Karpeles collected 1,612 tunes from 281 singers. Karpeles admitted that the two English collectors, working their way through the heart of Appalachia, were sometimes seen as "highly suspicious characters," in fact as German spies disguised as folk music collectors. Though they were hardly spies, the idea was not completely preposterous. And when world war again threatened, none other than the U.S. President decided it was an idea whose time had come.

4/musical Tradewinds

"I had come all this way on a quest of music.... The music was simply a delicious confusion, strangely sensuous and quite unfathomable art, mysteriously aerial, aeolian, filled with joy and radiance. Each night as the music started up I experienced the same sensation of freedom and indescribable freshness." —Colin McPhee

The years between the World Wars were heady ones for the growing cadre of songcatchers. Armed with the new microphones and disc machines that had ushered in the age of electric recording, they spread out across the globe, searching for musics that followed different paths from the Western sounds they were accustomed to, musics so powerful they transported listeners, brought on trance, gave the soul back its beat.

That musical quest had taken Densmore and Fletcher, Bartók and Sharp into the field, equipped with their wax cylinders and phonographs. As the Second World War approached, collectors had a new tool at their disposal— the Presto disc-cutter—and a yearning for what the French call a *connaissance du monde*, a knowledge of the world. In many ways, those between-the-wars songcatchers—artists, anthropologists, adventurers—were among the last great cultural explorers. For some of them, songcatching gave them what they craved most: the freedom of being a foreigner in a foreign land, immersed in a new culture.

But the exotic worlds that drew the songcatchers were beginning to crumble even as they found them, giving way under the weight of the very technologies that had produced better recording equipment and faster modes of travel. The planet was shrinking, homogenizing. By mid-century, new ideas, new politics, and new economies were sweeping across countries and continents. The gentle musical tradewinds that had blown for as long as humans had been making music were becoming a typhoon that would blow some musics into oblivion.

In 1935, two young brothers began a loudly publicized and far-flung collecting trip to the Pacific. Bruce and Sheridan Fahnestock were still in their 20s when they set sail for the South Seas on a 65-foot schooner, in part as an adventure and in part as an ornithological collecting expedition for the American Museum of Natural History. Their mother, Mary, went with them, and the spectacle of the swashbuckling young

[ABOVE] During a 1940 expedition to the South Seas, Bruce and Sheridan Fahnestock recorded Balinese music and that of other islands on the then state-of-the-art Presto disc-cutter. The Fahnestock collection eventually came to the Library of Congress, and in the early 1990s, the library's Endangered Music Project series digitized Fahnestock selections for its second CD— *Music for the Gods*.

[OPPOSITE] In Bali, where music seemed to flow like water, European and American music hunters converged in the 1930s and '40s, drawn by the haunting sounds of the gamelan and the graceful art of the dance.

> **1935**

New York's WNEW becomes first music and news radio station.

brothers flanking their portly, pearl-draped mother made the pages of major papers. "Schooner" Mary contributed to the hype with her book *I Ran Away to Sea at Fifty*, and the brothers chronicled their adventures, including pearl-diving escapades and escape from the Japanese during the Sino-Japanese War, in their own *Stars to Windward*.

Five years after that first expedition, the Fahnestocks were readying for another, much broader mission. Besides ornithological specimens for the American Museum, they wanted to collect the traditional music of the South Seas, hoping to record it before it was lost to Western influences and the rapid spread of Hawaiian-style guitar music. This time they had serious funding from a variety of sources, including NBC, which planned for the brothers to do live radio broadcasts to the American public even as they recorded island music.

On February 1, 1940, the Fahnestock's three-masted schooner, *Director II*, set sail from New York. "The loom of war stood prominently against the eastern horizon, and the smolderings lay in the West," Sheridan wrote dramatically in his memoirs. "With a tremendous sense of urgency the second Fahnestock South Seas Expedition headed toward the Pacific on a frigid winter morning in 1940." The crew of 23, mostly men in their 20s, included the indomitable Mary as well as anthropologist Jack Scott and ornithologist George Peterson. In eight months at sea, they covered 40,000 miles, making stops in the Marquesas, Tahiti, Fiji, Samoa, New Caledonia, and Australia. They collected bird specimens and music as they went and conducted oceanographic surveys

"The people…are happy indeed—there's no mistaking it in their songs, the old songs. The deep-throated raris are coming back and there are dances in the evening that haven't been seen since Herman Melville's time….And believe it or not, the war in Europe, ten thousand miles away, has done all this." —*Fahnestock Brothers*

Director II, a 147-foot fishing schooner that once roamed the Grand Banks, was refitted as a research vessel for the Fahnestock brothers' 1940 South Seas expedition.

[OPPOSITE] Mary Fahnestock (center) presides over a meal in the ship's main cabin, with her sons, their wives, and assorted crew members in attendance.

THE WHITE HOUSE
WASHINGTON

January 3, 1941.

MEMORANDUM FOR
GENERAL WATSON

I want to see Bruce and
Sheridan Fahnestock the
next time they are in
Washington, as I want to
hear all about their trip
to the South Seas.

F. D. R.

THE FAHNESTOCK SOUTH SEA EXPEDITION
FAHNESTOCK'S ZUID ZEE EXPEDITIE
FAHNESTOCK'S LAOETAN SELATAN SEMBERAP
OF
THE AMERICAN MUSEUM OF NATURAL HISTORY
CENTRAL PARK WEST AT 79TH STREET
NEW YORK, N. Y.

ADAM BRUCE FAHNESTOCK
JOHN SHERIDAN FAHNESTOCK
NETHERLANDS EAST INDIES
1941

PLEASE ADRESS REPLY:
c/o THE AMERICAN MUSEUM OF NATIONAL HISTORY
CABLE ADRESS "MUSEOLOGY NEW YORK"

Dear Mr. President:-

For six months we have worn a proud in-
signia in our hearts, a secret only for ourselves. We have
been President's Men. Now we are loathe to give up that
mark.

We went out to the Indies, studied Malay,
circulated among Dutch, half-castes, and natives, went the
length and breadth of Java, sailed to Madoera, Kangean, Bali,
Singapore, and Biliton, and found Borneo, the Celebes and
Moluccas closed to us.

In brief, quick points this is our impress-
ion. Some of this must certainly be repetition to you, but
that in itself may make the points stronger.

1. Native Unrest:- The half-caste and the
reasonably well-educated full blooded native wants a more
flexable government than the one supplied by Holland. This
movement is real and widespread. It is common talk everywhere
except among Dutch inhabitants who prefer to discount the whole
movement before foreigners. There has never been a Java-born
Governor General in the Indies and few Indies-born Dutch and
no native blood residents ever get higher in the government

of uncharted waters for the British and American navies. The brothers used two Presto disc-cutters to record remotely, taking to shore only a microphone, linked by as much as two miles of cable to the disc-cutter. Without obtrusive equipment, the brothers felt they got better coopera-tion from the performers and a higher-quality recording.

When the brothers were in Fiji, NBC managed to broadcast its only live recording session from the expedition. As planned, Bruce Fahnestock and his wife left the expedition there, with about 14 hours of recorded music in hand. In October, more of the 16-inch acetate discs were taken off the ship in Brisbane, Australia, and shipped to New York. This was fortuitous, because on October 18, off Gladstone, Queensland, the *Director II* ran aground on a shoal of the Great Barrier Reef and was soon shipping water.

The good people of Gladstone launched a rescue mission and crew and equipment were saved, but the *Director* was lost, and with it, all remaining plans for the expedition. Still, the Fahnestocks had recorded many hours of music, from the "deep-organ voices" of Samoans singing "ancient songs of great beauty," to the haunting sounds of Balinese gamelan orchestras, to Fijian legends, women's divination songs, harvest songs, and rice-pounding songs. They also found that some of the traditional musics had already been lost to missionary and colonial influences. But other music was making a comeback for an improbable reason. In a 1940s article for *Harpers* magazine, the brothers reported that in a deep valley in the Marquesas Islands, some old songs were being revived. They went on to explain that European ships had stopped coming to their island, and, left in peace, the islanders had returned happily to their traditional way of life.

In early 1941, with the war spreading, the brothers struck out on their third expedition, this time confined to Indonesia (then the Dutch East Indies). Once there, they chartered a sailboat and spent ten months recording in Bali, Java, Madura, and the Kangean Islands. What they brought back was a cache of traditional musics as yet untouched by war. But they collected more than music. "Both Bruce and I had spent the better part of 1941 in the East Indies ostensibly continuing the collection of primitive music, begun years before, but actually on a mission for President Roosevelt to measure the attitude of the Indonesians toward a possible invasion by the Japanese," wrote Sheridan Fahnestock in his unpublished memoirs.

In January 1942, the brothers' reputation and knowledge of the South Seas suddenly put them prominently on the military's radar screen. Sheridan got the first call: "My name is Arthur R. Wilson and I have been directed to take over a continent," said the caller, according to Fahnestock. "Will you command my small boats? Before you answer let me say that you must find the boats and find the crews. Such armament as can be provided is totally inadequate and unsuitable…. The name of the project is 'Mission X.'" The Fahnestocks' days as swashbuckling young songcatchers were forever over, but their travels—and boldness—summed up the era's romance of adventure.

At the same time that the American Museum of Natural History was funding amateur collectors like the Fahnestocks, it was sending out a cadre of scholars as well. While the brothers were sailing the South

[OPPOSITE] A letter to FDR—and his response—point out the significant role the Fahnestocks played in collecting cultural and political information in the South Seas. As war filled the Pacific, the Fahnestocks announced their third music-hunting expedition, this time to Indonesia. In truth, the brothers were on a covert mission for Roosevelt, designed to assess the local mood, defense facilities, and ability of small craft to be used effectively by American forces in the area. Though eminent anthropologist Franz Boas attacked scholars who "prostituted science by using it as a cover for their activities as spies," the practice was not uncommon during the war years. The Fahnestocks themselves went on to head up a motley armada of fishing trawlers, sailboats, and dories supplying Allied troops. Bruce Fahnestock lost his life early in the endeavor, but Sheridan became a highly placed officer under Douglas MacArthur. The brothers ragtag armada later inspired the 1960s television series, *The Wackiest Ship in the Army.*

Seas, a young anthropologist with the museum had been making a name for herself with her studies of Pacific Islanders. Margaret Mead was one of the new breed of anthropologists, trained by Boas and his protégée Ruth Benedict to study cultures comparatively in order to arrive at some understanding of human socialization and behavior on a global scale. In 1925, the 24-year-old Mead had set out for fieldwork in American Samoa, with instructions from Boas to study the Samoans and determine whether "the disturbances which vex our adolescents [are] due to the nature of adolescence itself or to civilization." Mead may not have answered that question for all time, but she did write her first classic, *Coming of Age in Samoa*, when she returned.

[ABOVE]   The glowing accounts of Balinese culture by composer Colin McPhee drew his friends, anthropologist Margaret Mead and her husband Gregory Bateson (top, in their "mosquito room" in the Sepik River region of New Guinea). Mead, who had studied cultures throughout the Pacific, admitted that fieldwork gave her the freedom "to strip off the layers of culturally attributed expected behavior and feel that one knew at last who one was."

She was soon back in the South Pacific, in Manus, and then in 1935 in Bali, with her third husband, British anthropologist Gregory Bateson. They had been drawn to Bali in part by what they had heard of it from composer Colin McPhee and his wife, anthropologist Jane Belo. By the time Bateson and Mead arrived, Bali held a well-established community of musicians and artists from Europe and America, who had discovered an island paradise where art seemed a staple of life and music was as great a necessity as food. "The sound of music seemed forever in the air," McPhee wrote in one of his many elegiac descriptions of the island. "People sang in the fields or in the streams as they

Chiming across the ocean, the Philippine nipple gong and other haunting instruments brought a rush of European and American musicians to the Pacific islands in the years between the wars.

bathed. From behind village walls rose the sound of flutes and cymbals ... at all hours of the day and night. Temples ... shook with the heavy beat of drums, the throb of enormous gongs ...."

As Mead and Bateson discovered, music was powerful for the Balinese. Some musical performances brought on trances, in which dancers and musicians were inhabited by gods who performed for the audience of mortals. Mead described "temple ceremonies in which the Witch is battled by the Barong, assisted by kris dancers who go into trance and stab themselves without injury," and "modern novelistic light operas which burlesque all the points of strain in the society" and shadow-plays—*wajangs*—with ornately painted puppets and *babats*, "the lovely musical tree which marks the beginning, the end and magic." But Mead could also see that modernization was creeping into this magic.

Bateson and Mead made voluminous photographs and films of the Balinese, but true to their training, they kept to their analytical roles as social scientists. McPhee, on the other hand, a musician himself, participated directly in Balinese music. Enraptured by it, he worked with Balinese musicians, helping to form a local gamelan club,

"It [Bali] is the most extraordinary combination of a relatively untouched native life going along smoothly and quietly in its old way with a kind of extraneous, external civilization superimposed like an extra nervous system.... But all this apparent 'civilization' is on the surface and Bali seems to have learned through a couple of thousand years of foreign influences just how to use and how to ignore those influences." —*Margaret Mead*

which was the standard way to begin forming an orchestra and train aspiring young musicians. He had the gongs and metal keys for the club's instruments "forged in one of the distant mountain villages to the east, long famed for their tuners ...," he wrote. "There was something dark and secret about their ancient craft, for they had to do with metal, cold mysterious produce of the underworld, charged with magic power.... In their craft the elements of life and death were strangely united. For a gong when struck can (or once could) dispel the demons, bring rain, wind; or give, when bathed in, health and strength...."

When McPhee played Western classical music on his phonograph for one gamelan musician, the man exclaimed, "Where is the beat? There is no beat! Like a bird with a broken wing!" Only jazz, McPhee wrote,

of leading figures in the arts world, and it was expatriate grande dame Gertrude Stein who suggested he and Copland go to the "dream city" of Tangier. "Like any Romantic," Bowles wrote, "I had always been vaguely certain that sometime during my life I should come into a magic place which, in disclosing its secrets, would give me wisdom and ecstasy—perhaps even death." Tangier would ultimately give him all those things.

Throughout his life, Bowles steadfastly refused to follow a predictable path. After a decade spent mostly in New York, composing ballets and scores for films and musicals by such leading lights as Orson Welles, William Saroyan, and Tennessee Williams, he turned his talents to writing his novel, *The Sheltering Sky*. Set in the Sahara, it reflected Bowles's fascination with the naiveté and helplessness of "civilized" Westerners when faced with the forces of more "primitive" traditions. As one critic explained, "Bowles has consistently searched its [civilization's] outermost fringes, the other side of the mirror." Bowles's idiosyncratic life, work, and personal style had made him a darling of the Beat Generation and the guru of the expatriate community. He probably cared little for this status. What he did care about, though, was a new passion: to record and preserve Moroccan folk music and lore. "To Europeans, the music of the Jilala is Moroccan folk music played on long, low-pitched transversal flutes and large flat hand drums," Bowles said "To a member of the cult, however, it is a sequence of explicit choreographic instructions, all of which are designed to bring about a state of trance, possession." One night, during a dinner party for Western journalists at Bowles's Tangier home, Mohammad Mrabet, the Moroccan storyteller whose work Bowles often recorded and translated, fell into a trance while listening to Jilala music and pulled out a long knife. Though he was subdued by men in the crowd, "it seemed unthinkable that anyone should have dared to interfere with a Moslem in a state of trance," Bowles wrote later, explaining that after Mrabet was tackled, the musicians had "played the necessary music until he was awake and able to speak."

In the last half of 1959, Bowles and two assistants set out across Morocco with an Ampex 601 tape recorder, because Bowles had become convinced that "the most important single element in Morocco's folk culture is its music…the entire history and mythology of the people is clothed in song." The trip was not easy, in part because the tape

[OPPOSITE] The movie version of Paul Bowles's literary masterpiece, *The Sheltering Sky*, featured the haunting music of Moroccan master musicians. Bowles's fascination with Moroccan culture revolved around its aural traditions, and he became committed to recording its music and legends.

> **1945**

U.S. Signal Corps captain Jack Mullin finds Magnetophones and magnetic tape in Radio Frankfurt and brings them back to America.

recorder required a 110-volt power source, often a rarity in the unelectrified villages of Morocco. But a result of the trip, Bowles's *Music of Morocco*, became a classic in the Library of Congress's Archive of Folk Song, and Bowles went on to record the sacred music of Moroccan Jews. Bowles died in Tangier in 1999, an increasingly obscure figure of a passed era. He told an interviewer late in his life, "I don't believe in free will. One does what one is fated to do. One is an onlooker watching life unfold—one's own and other peoples."

"I relish the idea that in the night, all around me...sorcery is burrowing its invisible tunnels in every direction.... Spells are being cast, poison is running its course.... There is drumming out there most nights. It never awakens me; I hear the drums and incorporate them into my dreams...and the dream goes on." —*Paul Bowles*

[OPPOSITE] A man of limitless creativity, Paul Bowles had composed an opera by the age of nine. He went on to create scores for Broadway and Hollywood productions—works Bowles called "functional music." For him, he said, the music of South America and Africa mirrored more closely his own philosophy and emotions.

THOUGH BOWLES HAD ULTIMATELY escaped New York, the intellectual ferment of the mid-century city unquestionably influenced him—as it did Mead and Bateson, McPhee and Belo. While Bowles composed and collected, New York activists wielded music as a tool, giving voice to otherwise unheard masses. One of these intellectual activists, Henrietta Yurchenco, seized the opportunity she had as a broadcaster on WNYC to air the sounds of "world folk and tribal music."

Proud of her reputation as a maverick, Yurchenco broke away from the predictable pop of the day and sought out and aired "weird" musics—the avant-garde works of European refugee composers (among them Béla Bartók), Indian sitar music, and the swelling voice of American folk music. "Towards the end of the 1930s," Yurchenco writes in her memoir, *Around the World in 80 Years*, "a colony of folk musicians from various regions settled in New York, primarily to raise money for political causes." Prominent among them were Woody Guthrie, Pete Seeger, Burl Ives, and Aunt Molly Jackson. "Unlike the popular songs...mostly about romantic love, their songs tracked every aspect of life from the history of their struggles to the intimate details of their private lives."

Though Yurchenco was not a musician herself, she understood the power of music to sway emotions and politics. In the early 1940s, disgusted by the rise of conservative American politics, she and her

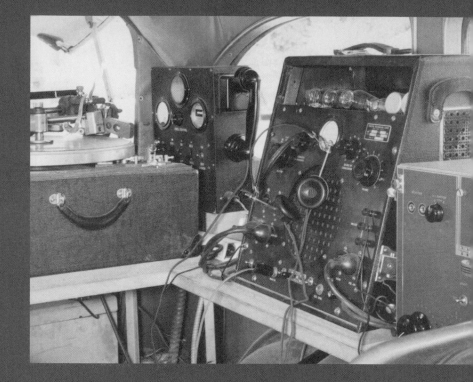

When Thomas Edison made his first tinfoil cylinder recording in 1877, it heralded a revolution in human communication.

SOUND CAPTURING

[BOTTOM] Edison's first phonograph recorded sound by making vertical impressions on tinfoil wrapped around a cylinder.

[OPPOSITE] By the mid-20th century, songcatchers like John and Alan Lomax were carting around carloads of equipment to make their field recordings.

For the first time in history, sound—all kinds of sound—could be preserved, however crudely, beyond the moment in which it was made. Just a couple of decades before, poet Emily Dickinson had written: "A word is dead / When it is said." Now a word—or song, or note—could potentially live forever.

But poetic sentiments were far from the driving force behind the inventions of Edison's age. At the turn of the last century, technological innovation dominated industry and the public consciousness as a torrent of new inventions and improvements on inventions flooded the marketplace. One of Edison's own employees, Nikolai Tesla, had discovered alternating electric currents, the system used to light the 1893 Chicago World's Fair. Alexander Graham Bell had perfected the technology for the telephone, and his cousin, Chichester Bell—along with Charles Tainter—had improved upon Edison's talking machine, using beeswax instead of tinfoil to coat a circular disk and a floating

stylus to incise it with vertical grooves. By 1885, their graphophone had been patented. Before the decade was out, one of Tainter and Bell's former employees, Émile Berliner, had entered the competitive fray, bringing out a gramophone that featured a flat, rubber vulcanite disc with lateral grooves. Berliner's flat disc made it infinitely easier to make multiple copies of a recording from a master disc. He soon replaced the vulcanite with shellac, the substance from which commercial records would be made for the next 50 years.

By the turn of the century, the vying recording companies were locked in litigation concerning patents on improvements. And the improvements were notable. Berliner's partner in the Victor Talking Machine Company, Eldridge Johnson, added a spring-driven motor to the gramophone and developed a tapered tone arm.

And as commercial records became more and more popular with the public, discs rapidly replaced cylinder recordings.

For field recordists, though, the cylinder phonograph offered distinct advantages: Relatively lightweight, it was portable and forgiving, as the wax from a bad recording could be shaved away and another recording made. Its disadvantages were shared by discs: As strictly acoustical devices, these early machines relied on mechanically recording sound through a single horn. All the singers or musicians recorded had to gather round a single horn to be "heard" by the machine, and neither the volume nor the frequency range could be manipulated.

Those drawbacks suddenly disappeared in the mid-1920s with the advent of electrical recording. The Warner Brothers Studios, in conjunction with Western Electric, propelled this giant leap forward. With the use of a microphone, rather than a horn, sound was

converted to electrical impulses—millivolts—that were then fed through a mike cable into an amplifier, which increased them to volts. The volts in turn went into a magnetic recording head that changed them back into acoustical vibrations that moved a needle and cut a disk. The process meant that volume and frequency range could now be manipulated and expanded. Sounds such as drumbeats, which occupied a frequency range beyond that picked up by acoustical recording, could at last be heard. And with the use of multiple mikes, several sound sources could be recorded simultaneously.

But another major innovation was in the offing, something that had been toyed with since the 19TH century—magnetic recording. In America, an inventor named Oberlin Smith succeeded in making magnetized recordings on steel wire the decade after Edison made his first cylinder recording. In 1898, Danish inventor Valdemar Poulsen patented the first magnetic recorder, also

using steel wire. But it would be three more decades before magnetic recording became a viable option, and that happened in Germany, where scientists pioneered a way of applying magnetic powder to paper or film to make magnetic tape. The Magnetophone had vastly improved fidelity over the scratchy sounds of the acetate-coated master discs used for recording, and the Germans put it to use recording propaganda for broadcast to the British.

In 1945, as the forces of the Third Reich retreated, American Signal Corps Capt. Jack Mullin, an electronics engineer, found two Magnetophones at the Radio Frankfurt station and brought them back to the U.S. Mullin understood the potential that magnetic tape held for the entertainment industry, and

he took the recorders to California, where they created an immediate sensation. By 1948, Ampex had brought out its Model 200 tape recorder for the U.S. market, and Bing Crosby was pioneering pretaped broadcasting for his popular radio show, with Jack Mullin as his chief engineer. In addition to its higher fidelity, tape allowed for smooth editing in ways that disc recordings never had.

For recordists in the field, new hardware opened up new possibilities, particularly when the Swiss-made Nagra appeared on the scene in the '50s. The brainchild of Polish physicist Stéfan Kudelski, this portable, self-contained audio recorder became the gold standard and continued to be a favored field recording device for many decades.

Edison's phonograph Experimental

[BOTTOM, INSERT] Émile Berliner's 1888 gramophone recorded sound on flat discs rather than cylinders. Disc recording would remain the industry standard for decades, until magnetic tape replaced it.

[OPPOSITE, INSERT] The mid-20th-century Nagra tape recorder gave field recordings an unprecedented fidelity.

Throughout the 1950s and '60s, rapidly improving recording and sound equipment flooded the commercial market—stereo LPs and tape; compact audio cassettes; car stereo systems and cassette players; and Dolby Noise Reduction. Then in the late '80s, the digital revolution swept through the marketplace and sound recording became computerized. Compact discs—CDs—replaced magnetic tape, and Surround Sound became a part of the home entertainment environment. For field recordists, DAT (Digital Audio Tape) recorders replaced the heavy bulk of the old Nagra. But the story that began a scant century ago with Edison and Tainter and Berliner and all the original sound innovators is far from over. It's anyone's guess how tomorrow will sound.

"I was at the center of all that was new and exciting in New York's musical scene in the pre-World War II years....I quickly acquired a reputation for weird programming...." —*Henrietta Yurchenco*

husband, artist Basil Yurchenco, moved to Mexico, where they found the artistic community and the government caught up in "an intense dedication to everything Indian." Supported by the government, Yurchenco soon found herself on the road, equipped with sound engineers, recording devices, even a car and driver. She had become a songcatcher.

But being a songcatcher in mid-century Mexico required serious commitment. Car travel was often impractical, since few real roads led to the remote areas that Yurchenco wanted to visit. A Mexican colleague warned her: "For a delicate woman like yourself, the road will be long and hard, and you can expect deadly insects, poisonous snakes, bad water, and no comforts at all."

It was a warning that female songcatchers had been hearing, in some form or other, for a half century. And like Alice Fletcher and others who had preceded her, Yurchenco ignored it.

Traveling to highland villages, she and her assistants sometimes went for weeks on donkeyback, lugging hundreds of pounds of equipment, often camping out and battling all the things her colleague had warned of, and more—flooded roads, bad-tempered dogs, worse-tempered scorpions, and unforgiving terrain. But the trips were also filled with almost idyllic beauty. "To avoid the heat we sometimes rode at night, especially when the moon was full," Yurchenco wrote. "These were among the most beautiful hours of all. Plants, cactus and trees, motionless in the pale blue light, had a mysterious aura that enhanced my sense of adventure." Sometimes villagers accused her of "stealing their music," even though she offered to pay, and sometimes the music was inauthentic, not worth recording. But Yurchenco knew she was often preserving something that would soon be lost.

Songcatching had become a passion, one that would lead Yurchenco back to Mexico time and again and would take her to other countries as well. In her travels, she recorded the musics of Spanish peasants, Morocco's Sephardic Jews, and the highlanders of Puerto Rico. And she has not stopped. From her apartment in New York, at festivals in Mexico and conferences in Central Europe, Yurchenco, now in her late 80s, still works tirelessly to promote the musics of the world.

Dutch musicologist Jaap Kunst gave the scholarly community the word ethnomusicology in 1950 to replace the term "comparative musicology." In academia, ethnomusicology was being recognized as a discipline in its own right. Still, 20TH-century songcatchers such as Yurchenco were an unusually diverse group with a variety of musical backgrounds. Laura Boulton, for instance, became one of the most visible ethnomusicologists of her time. Frequently pictured in newspaper and magazine articles with her microphone pointed at a "native" musician, Boulton was a well-connected woman who used her connections to great advantage, traveling the world in search of music. By her own reckoning, she participated in 28 recording expeditions to five continents in over 35 years of work.

Boulton, like many other ethnomusicologists, had been trained as a musician from childhood and had anticipated a career as a performer. But in the early 1930s she found herself shipping out for Africa as part

[ABOVE] Leaving behind New York and a career in radio broadcasting, Henrietta Yurchenco settled in Mexico in the early 1940s, just as appreciation for native Indian cultures was burgeoning.

[TOP] On an early field trip through Chiapas in 1942, Yurchenco recorded Tzotzil Maya musicians.

[OPPOSITE] Yurchenco's songcatching took her throughout Mexico, including Chihuahua, where she recorded a drummer of the Tarahumara in 1946.

of an American Museum of Natural History expedition. "It was Africa that provided for me the first exciting proof of what I had always believed to be true: that music is the most spontaneous and demonstrative form of expression the human family possesses...."

"I used to be introduced as a musical anthropologist or an anthropological musicologist. Now we have a word: ethnomusicologist."

—*Laura Boulton*

[OPPOSITE] On her first music-hunting expedition in the early 1930s, Laura Boulton ventured into Tanganyika's Nyasaland, where she recorded this local singer. When the man heard the cylinders played back, he declared: "Now I have heard myself sing, I would like to see myself dance"—a wish Boulton was unable to fulfill.

> **1951**

Polish physicist Stéfan Kudelski invents the Nagra, a portable recording machine that will revolutionize field recording.

On that first expedition, Boulton supped with African kings, went on a photo safari with Denys Finch Hatton, immortalized in Isaak Dinesen's *Out of Africa*, and, above all else, searched for music. "From morning until night, from cradle to grave, everything is done to the rhythm of a song. Whether sharpening his knife, paddling his canoe, or making a sacrifice to his gods, [the African] performs his task to the accompaniment of music," Boulton wrote. She explained that, because of the critical role of rhythm, "Africans...have developed the drum more fully than any other people...." She even described seeing young boys playing two drums at once, with a different rhythm for each hand.

From her first trip to Africa, Boulton was hooked. Music and folkways became a passion, and she collected all over the world. In India, she battled her way into a *kumba mehla*, a pilgrimage attracting literally a million devotees to the headwaters of the Ganges. She overcame an earthquake and floods to get to Tibetan monasteries; she made her way to Nepal, Southeast Asia, Japan. She recorded the rare liturgical music of Orthodox monasteries, the chants of Inuit in Hudson Bay, and vodun ceremonies of Haiti. She befriended Indian maharajas and Zen masters and such legendary figures as Haile Selassie, the Lion of Ethiopia, and Albert Schweitzer, the great humanitarian and authority on Bach. Boulton visited Schweitzer at his famous hospital in Lambaréné, French Equatorial Africa, in 1956, and at last recorded the music the doctor had decades before implored the Berlin Phonogramm-Archiv to preserve.

In her long career, Boulton used cylinder recorders, discs, and magnetic tape in her songcatching, and she sometimes took a cameraman with her, bringing back live footage along with her audio recordings. Boulton's years of firsthand experience with different musics gave her a rich understanding of the many ways that humans make and use music, and the ways that musics are lost. "Musicologists today often

Jungle Safer Than City to Her

Miss Boulton's Planning a New Expedition

By BARBARA BIGELOW.

Exploring the Arctic or equatorial Africa is a health cure compared to life in Manhattan for the past two months. Take it from Laura Boulton, young woman explorer who weathered nine expeditions with nary a sniffle and is now battling a bad cold in her 53rd St. apartment.

"Every time I get back to New York, the pressure and the pace of things have gotten worse," she says between coughs. "I suppose it's because you deal more with universals out in the field and life is simpler."

Come summer, Miss Boulton expects to be off again on another expedition. That it will be a large project, extending over several continents and years, is all that she can say just now. There's as much difficulty finding tents, grills and exploring paraphernalia in the stores these days as nylons.

Collects Native Music.

Though she has been in many places where no other white woman ever was, Miss Boulton's main interest is the music of primitive peoples rather than staking out claims to new peaks or lands. Over the past 17 years she has made comprehensive collections and recordings of native music from the French Sudan to the east Arctic. The RCA-Victor Co. is publishing 10 albums of her work.

"Interest in a people's music is the quickest means to understand them," Miss Boulton emphasizes. "It's a far more productive way than the old question-and-answer method. In many African tribes music rules everything they do; sharpening knives, paddling canoes, childbirth, and religious rites."

Drum orchestras which reach tremendous complexities of rhythm are common in Africa. On a music project for the Canadian government covering 45 nationalities in 1941, Miss Boulton found Scottish music on Cape Breton in a more ancient form than exists today in Scotland.

"They have a kind of psalmody where a precentor starts the theme and the chorus answers afterwards, which I doubt is found anywhere else in the world," she says.

First Safari in 1929.

A native of Ohio, the attractive explorer made her first safari in 1929 with her husband. This was the Straus Central African expedition for the American Museum of Natural History. Others included the Carnegie Museum South African expedition, the Pulitzer Angola trip, the Mandel West Indies expedition for the Field Museum, the Crane Mexican expedition for the Museum of Modern Art in 1940. Two years later she was leader of a Canadian-Arctic trip which made the first color film of life in the east Arctic.

Just now Miss Boulton is wearing a chic up-do and a fringe of sculptured curls on her brow. Asked if this effect could be maintained on ice floes and in the veldt, she said:

"Heavens, no. I hack it off to about three-inches length all 'round before I go on a trip. Then I can whip a comb through it and only do it up on pins every now and then."

Safer than City.

A cry cry from the weatherbeaten, knickered woman explorer, Miss Boulton is slim and svelt with a peaches-and-cream complexion. She has an irreverent approach to explorers who spin harrowing tales of being lost in jungles and charged by rhinos. If you keep your head and use common sense, an expedition is safer than life in New York, she maintains.

Now that the war has ended, the veteran explorer expects a rash of scientific trips to break out. She advises any girl anxious to affiliate with an expedition to develop a technique which will fit in with the purpose of the group.

"You can't just barge into an expedition," she warns. "Get expert in photography, music or botany and find work in a topflight museum for background. Once you are taken on, remember that the most important attitude to have is one of respect for things that other cultures hold sacred. Just because people are primitive doesn't mean that you can go in and grab what you want from them."

Laura C. Boulton.

Beside a branch of the old Chisholm Trail, on the Bosque River bottomland where the Lomaxes settled, cowboys roamed, while Scandinavian immigrants and newly freed blacks struggled, like the Lomaxes, to wrest a living from the land. Racial prejudices still ran deep here, as did a confirmed belief in the many opportunities of America. It was on this robust Texas ground that young John Lomax, James's sixth son, grew up.

Alan Lomax and his father, John, would help reshape American music, bringing the sounds of folksingers and bluesmen like Wilson Jones [BELOW] and fiddler Wayne Perry to a broader public audience.

[OPPOSITE] "As picturesque and belligerent a vagabond as I ever saw... but clean inside and out," a family friend once said of the young Alan Lomax.

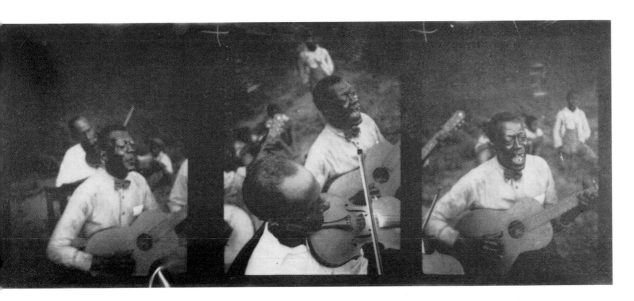

By the time he was about to turn 40, John could claim some success as a college administrator at the University of Texas, then as an English professor at the newly formed Texas A&M. But things were about to change for him. In the summer of 1906 he left his familiar Texas surroundings and went to Harvard on a year-long teaching fellowship. While there, he caught the attention of the great English scholar George Lyman Kittredge, who, like his predecessor Francis James Child, was the acknowledged expert in folk songs—which at that time meant mostly English and Scottish ballads. But Lomax intuitively understood that the cowboy songs of his native region were their own brand of folksinging, and his proposal to collect them intrigued the Harvard academics. If this self-styled Texas cowboy could pull off his idea, the notion of what constituted folk music and what was worth collecting might open out in a whole new direction.

And he did pull it off, publishing *Cowboy Songs and Other Frontier Ballads* in 1910. Lomax put together the songbook, which contained such then-unknown gems as *Home on the Range*, by sending out circulars requesting

> **1927**

Ralph Peer stages the legendary Bristol Sessions in Tennessee, inviting local talent to record for the Victor company.

Tuned up, the Steele family of
Hamilton, Ohio, performs for
Alan Lomax's microphone in 1938.

Library of Congress
Washington, D. C.
February 4, 1941

Mr. Woody Guthrie
General Delivery
Columbia, California

Dear Woody:

I haven't had much time to take it easy since your letter came or
to do any letter-writing either. Besides "School of the Air" and
"Back Where I Come From", I am working every day on a really good
folk song program with my father, who should have been hired by
Columbia years ago instead of me to talk about folk songs. We are
putting him and his recordings on a series of transcribed records
for distribution to the stations all over the country and he really
takes it slow and makes it juicy.

Would you mind us using your record of "Whoopee Ti Yi Yi Yo" and
"Get Along Little Dogie", which Father thinks is pretty fine?

I really miss you a lot on "Back Where I Come From". The program
has become very "merry" and "jolly" since you left us. We don't
have anybody who can come out and speak his mind with sincerity and
honesty the way you can. Pete is on very regularly and his banjo
playing adds a lot. Direction has improved a great deal and everyone
likes the show except maybe Burl who is beginning to feel his oats
these last days.

The tower finally got too high for us when the winter wind really
began to blow and we've retreated into town in an apartment that's
so snug it's practically underground, the address being 912 19th
Street N.W. if you and your family are ever along that way or should
care to drop me a line.

I don't know what to do about the Tom Joad song myself since I am
also in the business but I am going to call up Steinbeck's agents and
see whether they won't take action for you. It seems to me they are
the proper people to handle it. If I did anything myself it would
appear that I had a personal grudge against Siegmeister, which I don't.
I'll tell them to write you direct about it.

I hope you are going to work more on your writing and get those short
stories written. When they are ready I'll show them to everybody I
know and try to help get them sold if you would like me to. I believe
your job in the world is as a writer as well as a talker and singer,
and I hope you keep digging at it.

Give my regards to your family and to California and to those miners
who know how to take it easy.

Yours,

Alan Lomax

he should be receiving royalties at all—an issue frequently ignored by early songcatchers.

In 1950, Lomax picked up his tape recorder and headed for Europe. For the next eight years he would do there what he had done in America—record the greatest folk musicians he could find in the British Isles, Spain, and Italy and broadcast some of their music on the BBC's *Third Programme*. He believed passionately that if the folk musicians he was recording could hear their works on the radio, they would regain confidence in their own traditions.

Lomax returned to America with an even bigger vision for music and humankind than he had had when he left. He had developed a theory that a particular culture's music and dance could be correlated with other social factors. His cantometrics system relied on 37 scales that charted various aspects of a song's performance. These would, he felt, show a cross-cultural correlation with other social conditions. So, for example, nasality in singing would predominate in societies where sexual repression of females was the norm. Later, using the principles of cantometrics, he developed the Global Jukebox, a multimedia database of thousands of songs and dances.

Lomax also contributed to songcatching in a different way by promoting and publicizing the Swiss-made Nagra tape recorder. "It is the best field recorder for folk music that I have come across—rugged, hi-fi, easy to operate, and unaffected by temperature, dust, etc.," he wrote. The battery-operated Nagra, compact and portable at 18 pounds, was to become an indispensable tool for field-workers.

In the end, Lomax was driven by a single idea—and fear—that underlay all his others:

"Every smallest branch of the human family at one time or another has carved its dreams out of the rock on which it has lived.... Each of these ways of expressing emotion has been the handiwork of generations of unknown poets, musicians and human hearts. Now, we of the jets, the wireless and the atomblast are on the verge of sweeping completely off the globe what unspoiled folklore is left.... and variety is in danger of being replaced by a comfortable but sterile and sleep-inducing system of cultural super-highways—with just one type of diet and one available kind of music." —*Alan Lomax*

[OPPOSITE] A 1941 letter from Alan Lomax to Woody Guthrie touches on many of the concerns the two faced: Alan's programming for his radio show and Woody's own battles for copyright to his songs. Guthrie, Pete Seeger, Burl Ives, Lomax's sister Bess, and others began the influential folk group, the Almanac Singers, in the politically charged climate of late 1930s New York. By the late 1940s, the group had evolved into the popular Weavers.

On some level, a similar belief inspired the work of a Polish émigré to America. Moses Asch, son of the prominent Jewish writer Sholem Asch, was born in Warsaw in 1905, as political unrest and violence disrupted life there. Five years later, in 1910, his family left Europe and settled in New York. Even as a teenager, Moe's passion was for sound and he became an avid ham radio operator, with a precocious talent for electronics. Back in Europe for schooling in his late teens, Asch stumbled on a copy of John Lomax's *Cowboy Songs and Other Ballads* in a book stall along the Seine. To Asch, it was proof that America had its own unique voices.

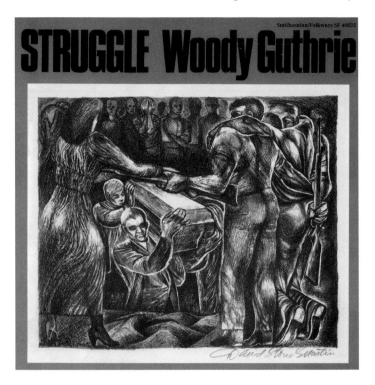

When Asch returned to the U.S. soon thereafter, commercial radio was coming into its own. Never before had a household been able to tune into a larger world, connecting to others via invisible waves, creating for the first time in history a broadcast mass medium. The phonograph had allowed for sound transmission a dollop at a time, but broadcast technology would change the face of America, and eventually the world. An engineer at heart, the young Asch made radio his career—working briefly for the fledgling RCA corporation cataloguing parts, then repairing radios on his own. In 1938 his small business, Radio Labs, was hired to record music for the Yiddish radio station, WEVD. And so Moe Asch turned his engineering talents to studio recording, at first focusing on predominantly Jewish music but gradually expanding into the burgeoning jazz and folk scene that swirled through New York in the '30s and '40s.

In the early 1940s Leadbelly, long since eclipsed in the popular mind by newer sounds, showed up at Asch's studios, and immediately the two men "were brothers," according to Asch. "I understood him, he understood me…. He was a great intellect. A real, hard-thinking practical man…." Over the next decade Asch released a number of Leadbelly recordings. At the same time he began recording such jazz greats as Mary Lou Williams and reissuing the classical works of European artists, including Béla Bartók. (Béla's son Peter would later become Asch's respected sound and recording engineer.) But his studio gained

In the early 1950s, the legendary Folkways label released albums by bluesmen like Brownie McGhee, as well as by leading voices of the folk revival like Woody Guthrie and Pete Seeger. "Folkways set itself a boundless mission," *New York Times* music critic Jon Pareles wrote, "it would record everything in the world that's worth hearing…except the commercial pop that pays…bills."

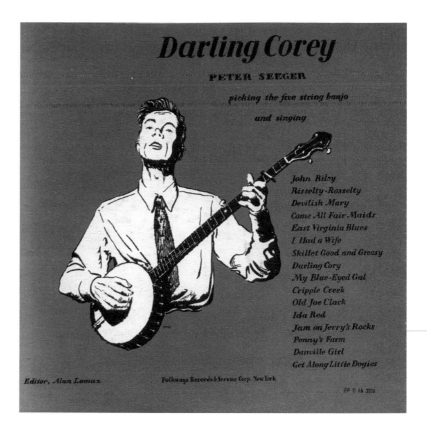

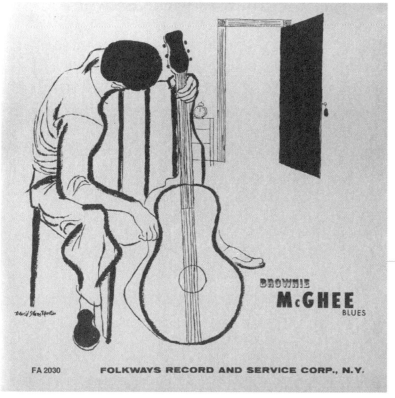

MUSIC AND POLITICS: A POWERFUL MIX

[ABOVE] A Nazi rally uses music and fanfare to rouse passions.

[RIGHT] Singer-songwriter Woody Guthrie wrote such classics as "This Land is Your Land" and "Tom Joad" to inspire workers, farmers, African Americans, and all those he considered oppressed to claim their rights.

> "Give me the making of the songs of a nation and I care not who makes its laws."
>
> —*Andrew Fletcher, 18TH-century Scottish political philosopher*

If music were not a powerful resource in social and political struggles, it would not be so widely censored, controlled, and surrounded with restrictions. Musicians would not be so suspect, so often imprisoned, and so frequently silenced. Music creates loyalties and galvanizes opposition so well that music itself sometimes becomes an object of struggle.

Although not found in all societies, political song has been a staple of European and American political action for centuries. Before the Revolutionary War, American colonists wrote ballads lambasting the British and the King of England. In fact, Peter Zenger, the newspaper publisher in New York City whose case is credited with establishing freedom of the press, was imprisoned by the British for publishing ballads and anonymous essays critical of the British Governor. When war began, Americans fought to the sound of fifes and drums and improvised verses of "Yankee Doodle." In the Civil War and later conflicts, "When Johnny Comes Marching Home Again" and "Battle Hymn of the Republic" moved them. But they also marched against war, singing "Gonna Study War No More," and they marched for Civil Rights, singing "We Shall Overcome." Picket lines were mobilized to the tune of "Which Side Are You On?" and common bonds expressed with "This Land is Your Land."

From John Adams's election campaign ("Adams and Liberty") through about 1948 ("I'm Just Wild About Harry"), every presidential election gave songwriters an opportunity to practice their craft. Political parties published their own songbooks and encouraged supporters to sing together at rallies, as did labor unions and farmers' movements. Enslaved Africans and their descendants also used songs to express their feelings and articulate their hopes—though often in a veiled way, for racism and repression continued to be severe long after emancipation. Spirituals, blues, work songs, lullabies, and other genres were used to give voice to their struggles and protests.

The rise of the European nation-states in the 19TH century was often bolstered by the discovery or creation of a national musical style. Scholars and composers in many countries began to turn to the local, or "folk," traditions for inspiration. This wedding of folk traditions and politics happened somewhat later in the United States, where the urban elite managed to combine a celebration of American culture with a strong political message. Music was seen as a means to change the nature of society itself. In 1934, Charles Seeger wrote that art "is a social force. It is propaganda.... The better the art, the better propaganda it makes: the better the propaganda the better art it is."

Encouraged by nationalist trends and by the Communist International, which recommended the use of local forms to express revolutionary content, many politically committed musicians began to seek out rural musicians and to arrange their materials for urban audiences. Charles Seeger and Elie Siegmeister composed avant-garde political music this way, while Alan Lomax encouraged a number of musicians to use their creative talents for political ends and composed some pieces of his own in a more "folk" idiom.

Dozens of political songbooks were published by the Socialist Party, the IWW, and other organizations in the opening decades of the 20TH century—one of the most famous being the 1935 *Rebel Songbook*, which included the "International" and Joe Hill's "The Preacher and the Slave." "A singing army is a winning army and a singing labor movement cannot be defeated," Labor Union President John L. Lewis said. "When hundreds of men and women in a labor union sing together, their

individual longing for dignity and freedom are bound into an irrepressible force."

The 1930s saw a flowering of political music. Building on the work of Joe Hill and other activist composers who had set new words to popular tunes, songwriters like Woody Guthrie, Earl Robinson, Pete Seeger, and many immigrant songwriters composing in their own languages and musical idioms used songs to express political opinions and move people to action.

Although the McCarthy era devastated the careers of many composers and performers, it did not end the use of music as a tool to change society. The American Civil Rights movement used music systematically as a mobilizing force and popularized such songs as "We Shall Overcome" and "Oh, Freedom." The 1960s and 1970s saw music emerging as the public face of a number of national and international political movements. American songwriters turned their attention to the Vietnam War

with the "I-Feel-Like-I'm-Fixin-to-Die Rag" and other protest songs. Bob Marley championed freedom and human rights through his danceable reggae. In Latin America, musicians of Nueva Cancion, such as Victor Jara, wrote ballads for local musical instruments and were killed or exiled for their efforts. "The term 'protest song' has been oversimplified …," Pete Seeger once said. "A lullaby is a propaganda song in the opinion of a three year old child who doesn't want to be put to sleep."

In the 1980s rap musicians took a tradition of street rhymes and forged a style that has spread around the world—often (but certainly not always) as a protest against injustice. In this, rap resembles many other genres that have spread political messages over the past few hundred years.

Not all protests have been from the political left; not all musical propaganda seeks to change the fundamental structures of society. Music is also used to sell products from soft drinks to cars to foreign policy. (In 2002 the United States government crafted special musical radio programming to "win hearts and minds" in Afghanistan.)

Music has been an effective resource for social movements because of the variety of ways it can be used—with subtlety or bluntness—and its ability to be made or listened to while doing other things. Forged, transformed, and sometimes abandoned in the crucible of struggles, music is part of the complex web of sounds and signs with which we experience and make history.

ANTHONY SEEGER
Department of Ethnomusicology
University of California at Los Angeles

ntury folksingers whose progressive
made. Woody Guthrie, the Dust
of the Asch label, and Pete Seeger
workers movement, also recorded

Moe could do what he wanted,
artists he respected free rein.
. They would drop by his studio
ecording sessions, with Asch him-
the spring of 1943, Asch Studios
reative energy, a number of leg-
ord—Guthrie and Leadbelly, Mary
White, Blind Sonny Terry and Bess
ven a gospel singer.

machinery
We tried
nd whoops
and buggy
and Marian
h their plate glass

, Asch would bring out countless ground-
one to be motivated by commercial success,
sed of looking for the most esoteric musics
is partnership with ethnographer Harold
d an Ethnic Series for his now renowned Folk-
an in the early 1950s when his previous studio
would later be known as "world music" had
by mid-century. Prior to the Folkways record-
h as that recorded by Laura Boulton, was
d by major labels, and that generally as a tax
nic Series would eventually bring the musics
m all over the world to an American audience.

n failing health, began looking for a buyer
on he had amassed over almost half a century.
see the deal concluded, the Smithsonian

With his usual hands-on approach, Folkways impresario Moe Asch oversees a recording session in his New York studio.

Institution bought the collection soon after his death in 1986 and continues to honor Asch's stipulation that all the music he had produced be available in perpetuity. As he liked to say about the esoteric music he recorded, "The letter Q isn't used much, but that doesn't mean it shouldn't be part of the alphabet."

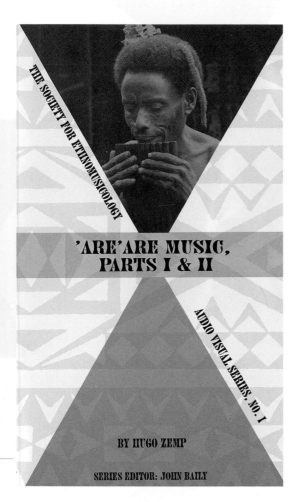

In his groundbreaking 1970s film on the 'Are'are of the Solomon Islands, Swiss scholar Hugo Zemp used native experts to reveal the extraordinary richness of a complex, polyphonic music unknown until then. A major figure in ethnomusicology today, Zemp has done pioneering work on many musical traditions and edits the renowned Le Chant du Monde series of the world's musics. [OPPOSITE] A 1960s Zemp photograph of a Mandango female drummer—a rare occurence in Côte d'Ivoire

Born into a world where recordings were made on wax cylinders and radio had not yet been heard of, Asch left one where sound engineering could accomplish virtual miracles and commercial recording had become part of the fabric of industry. In this more sophisticated world, the scholars—now with the official title of ethnomusicologists—continued to analyze music for its structure and its cultural resonance. With portable tape recorders, field recording was more reliable and the fidelity much greater. And a few scholars began to realize that they could now add a new dimension to their musical documentation—film.

Hugo Zemp was a classical, conservatory-trained percussionist when he went to Africa in 1958 to spend time with the drummers of Côte d'Ivoire, particularly the Dan people. While there, he met a French couple—the husband an ethnographer and the wife an ethnomusicologist—who broadened his focus beyond just the music to its cultural import. When Zemp returned to Europe, he soon found himself on a path far from the concert halls of the West, breaking new ground with his book *Musique Dan* and his West African recordings. In the 70s, he went to the Solomon Islands, enticed there by the pan pipe music of the 'Are'are. But Zemp did more than record their music. He filmed the 'Are'are making it and added to the film the many cultural elements that went into music—from the instruments to the complex social interactions that came together around the music. His 'Are'are work did more than earn him academic awards; it inspired him to expand the place of film in the study of music.

In 1989, Zemp broke ground again in a film he did on biphonic singing. Using a spectrogram format, he showed how the vocal overtones behaved, as one heard the sounds synchronized with the graphic image. He also filmed in remote Swiss valleys, where ancient

traditions of yodeling were still practiced. And he returned to
Côte d'Ivoire to make films and recordings of the balafon and
xylophone music of the Senufo people.

> "Music is not just sound. It's movement, it's dance, it's the relationship
> among the musicians, and the musicians and the dancers, and the
> musicians and dancers and audience. It's related to ritual and work
> and social interaction." —*Hugo Zemp*

While Zemp translated his passion for music into an academic pursuit,
a classically trained pianist in New York used her talents to reach a
broader audience. A child prodigy, Tracey Sterne eventually gave up
the stage and became immersed in the recording industry. In 1969, she
left Vanguard, a label that recorded some of the same musicians as
Moe Asch's Folkways, and moved to Nonesuch records. In her 14 years
there, Sterne took what Asch had begun a step further, opening the
horizons of commercial recording well beyond what was considered
safe and acceptable.

"Mainstream is such an old-fashioned concept. Our public is interested in every kind of music and that interest laps over into far more than just music." —*Tracey Sterne*

Under Sterne, Nonesuch pursued innovative new composers, engineered the ragtime revival of the '70s, and pioneered the Explorer Series, bringing out an eclectic offering of musics from around the world—from Bali to the Himalaya to Latin America. "Tracey had a gift for responding with perception to just about any music that was thrown at her. She had the rare ability to treat music from an unfamiliar culture as music, not as a curiosity. If it was good music, it was good music," David Lewiston, her collaborator on the Explorer Series, said. The 70-some albums in the series also inspired Western musicians to meld other musical traditions into their own creations. Nonesuch has announced plans recently to rerelease Explorers titles on CDs.

Tracey Sterne, the visionary behind Nonesuch Records from 1965 to 1979, spearheaded the growing popular interest in the world's musics with her Explorers Series.

Lewiston, too, was a classically trained pianist and made his first field recordings on a trip to Bali in 1966. On a whim, he took the recordings to Sterne, and, hearing them, she wanted them on the spot. They became the haunting *Music from the Morning of the World*. The peripatetic Lewiston would make a total of 28 recordings for the Nonesuch Explorer Series. "I'd call Tracey from the airport whenever I landed in New York with new recordings, and I'd say 'See you in an hour.' She generally produced what I'd recorded in my rambling," he said.

Sterne understood not just how broad the human range of music-making was but also the public's capacity to appreciate and absorb all kinds of musics. It was no longer just the scholars and the musicians and the lovers of the exotic who could hear and respond to the music of the "other." Sterne and other pioneers of the recording industry proved that musiclovers everywhere would enjoy—and buy—music from other cultures.

In the Himalaya foothills of Hunza, David Lewiston (left) records a local *bitaah*—shaman—singing his way into trance. A regular on the Nonesuch Explorer Series, Lewiston made field recordings throughout Asia and Latin America in the 1970s.

6 / Long, strange Trip

It was a hot time in the late '60s in San Francisco. The street was alive with Hell's Angels, hippies, the SLA, and the diggers. People were casting off the '50s, cutting the cord, and a new culture was springing up from the chaos of the street.

"Psychedelic cowboys," the Grateful Dead pose in front of the Barn, their Novato, California, hideaway in the late 1960s. The band coalesced around lead guitarist Jerry Garcia (center), becoming a major force in Bay Area music. Mickey Hart (second from right) became the Dead's percussionist in 1967.

The Grateful Dead, the Jefferson Airplane, Janis, Big Brother, and the Quicksilver Messenger Service were discovering a new musical topography, a new blend of psychoactive life. We were explorers on the edge, circumnavigating this brave new world. There were no rules. Everywhere you turned people were making things happen. Smoking grass, taking acid, turning on. It was wild on wild, sunrise till sunset, and on till dawn. Days on end, losing sleep—all this cut loose your moorings from the everyday world.

I had just finished four years in the Air Force and landed in the middle of this rush of creative joy. Music and art were everywhere. I couldn't wait to get up in the morning, go to the Potrero Theatre, and jam. For the Dead, an all-day rehearsal was not unusual. My mind would be spinning out of control, my hands aching, my young body supplying the energy for endless creativity. We were making a new culture and a new music, and we were doing it at the spiritual, geographical, and cultural edge of America.

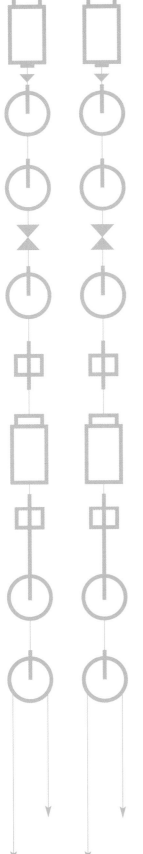

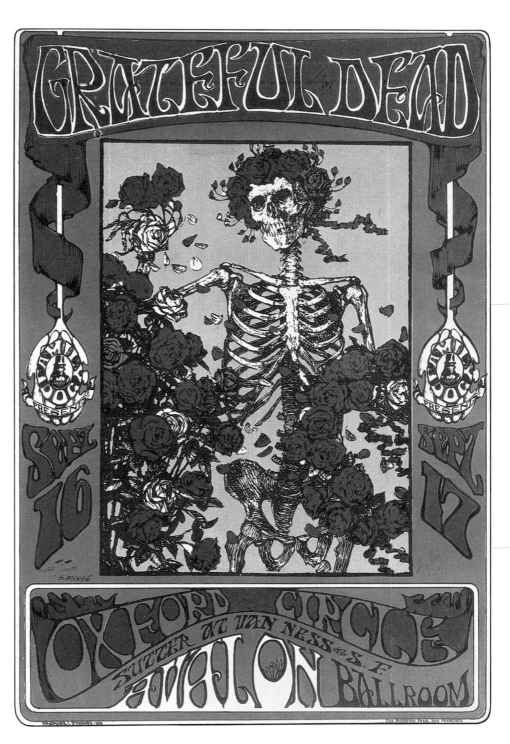

I knew that I was exactly where I should be in this experience/experiment. The San Francisco Bay Area was alive with new ideas and new art. It also hosted some very old art—particularly North Indian classical music—transplanted to American soil. In the middle of my own drumming to wild crowds at the Fillmore, I realized that some of the best musicians on the planet were drifting, almost invisibly, into the area, playing in small theaters. The sound was terrible in those places—they had feedback, bad speaker systems, and no qualified PA operators. There were few people here anyway who could understand the complex North Indian sound—one of the most muscular and rhythmically intricate musics I had experienced. I fell in love with it, its rhythms took me into a deep trance.

When I went to the record stores looking for Indian music, I found little of it, and what I did find was poorly recorded. Then it dawned on me that this was my mission. I would offer my services in the name of good sound and good recording, delivering the sound system free of charge and recording the music, just for them and for me. I could record Ali Akbar Khan on sarode, Sultan Khan on sarangi, and Sachdev on flute. There was Zakir Hussain and his father, the great tabla master Alla Rakha. All masters, all here in San Francisco. I couldn't believe how fortunate I was. I had the spare equipment from the Grateful Dead's sound system at my disposal, and I had my tool of choice—a Nagra.

> **1969**

Dolby Noise Reduction improves the quality of prerecorded tape.

At that time most recordings were made at 7.5 ips (inches per second). With tape moving at that speed, I couldn't achieve the quality I wanted. I was a purist, a collector. It had to be right. I began to roll tape at twice that speed, at 15 ips. This was uncommon for field recordings in those days. Tape was expensive, I had little money even for food, and Indian performances could go on for many hours. But this was a chance of a lifetime, and I was determined not to lose it. I expect these remarkable musicians thought I was a bit crazy.

Ravi Shankar asked if there were other American musician/recordists like me. I laughed and said I didn't think so.

After a night of glorious recording, I would drive as fast as I could back to the Grateful Dead's sanctuary, our ranch in Novato. I'd rush in, unpack, and put the fresh tape on the Nagra as my heart raced in anticipation. I'd sit in my green chair—a sonic throne reserved

strictly for listening—and let myself slide into this silken music, waves of sound washing over me, caressing me. I was an aficionado, and all I wanted for my efforts was to listen to that music, to take it out and bathe in it any time. I was like an art collector who keeps masterworks in his private vault.

I always sat in my listening chair. I had found it at a flea market, all broken down, torn, and ugly. When I set my eyes on it, I knew it would serve me well. It was the same kind of chair Grandfather had had in our living room when I was a boy. He would sit there when he came home from work and read the *New York Times*, cover to cover. Then he would watch Walter Cronkite on the evening news. In the afternoons when Grandfather wasn't home, I would crawl up in his chair and listen to Pygmy recordings over and over again. Now, in San Francisco, the green listening chair that I found was my link to the time when I first became a searcher for the sounds of the world. Those days in Grandfather's chair were to prove critical to my future as a recordist.

Master of the Indian tabla, Zakir Hussain (left) plays with Latin percussionist Giovanni Hidalgo. Hussain's father, Ustad Alla Rahka—also a tabla master—took Mickey Hart from Western drumming to another percussive dimension: "Rhythm is just time," according to Alla Rahka, "and time can be carved up any way you want."

In 1978, the Grateful Dead played three charitable concerts at Egypt's Great Pyramids. The Bedouin who gathered in the desert to listen added their traditional wailing to the rock'n roll.

[OPPOSITE] While in Egypt, Hart pursued his field recording—taping, among other things, the music of the felucca boatmen.

I went from being a music maker to being a music collector. It became an overwhelming passion. I would seek out all music that was unrecorded or recorded badly, music that stirred my soul and drew me into its web. If you looked hard enough, this music was everywhere. I had the notion that San Francisco was located on a musicothermal hot spot, emitting an energy that attracted creative forces. I was sitting on the mountaintop, and I knew it.

In 1978 the Grateful Dead played at the foot of the Great Pyramids in Cairo. Everyone took his or her mate or friends. I took my Nagra. I knew the wide-open desert of North Africa was filled with music that fueled living. The desert was not just empty miles of sand and oases; it contained thousands of years of nomadic traditions. There was the music of the Nile and the music of the cabarets that dotted the towns and villages of that great river. And there was the music of the deep desert. It was music influenced by the Arab diaspora of the 11TH, 12TH, 13TH, and 14TH centuries. As the Arab warrior-traders crossed the Arabian Peninsula and spread west, they left their mark on North Africa, infusing the desert with their music and culture.

After playing the pyramid gigs with the Grateful Dead, I packed up my Nagra and decided to head south along the Nile to Aswan. Aswan was where I would find the music of the people who sailed the waters in their feluccas. As they swept back and forth across the Nile, they sang sailing songs. I made friends with a captain and asked him if I could record the crew's songs. He agreed, and a deal was struck. I chartered a boat, and we sailed and sailed until my batteries ran out.

A curious thing happened that day. As the sun set, I started to think of my green listening chair and how good it would be to have it there that night. At that moment, I realized that this music should go beyond me in my small world. It should be heard by everyone.

After the Nile, it was off to the coastal desert. I hired an Egyptian guide, set out for Alexandria, and wound up at a wadi in the Sahara. This was the Egypt of my dreams. Endless sand dunes wound down to Alexandria, the center of learning in the ancient world. Two thousand years ago, when ships came into port here, their cargoes of papyrus and scrolls were confiscated and put into the great library of Alexandria. Out in the desert, somewhere, were the nomadic tribes who traversed this expanse. What did they sound like? How was I going to find them? *Go to a bar*, I thought, *meet the people, ask questions.*

One evening in a bar, as the drinks and conversation flowed, the locals asked about the strange machine I was carrying around. One fellow I was getting to know—Hani Sabat—had a house on the outskirts of town, at the edge of the desert, and he invited me to stay there that night and tell him all about America. He said he was a merchant. I didn't press him, as I got the feeling he didn't want to reveal the commodity he dealt in. No problem. We stayed up all night, talking about his life, my life, drinking, smoking hashish, and becoming friends. The conversation finally turned to my main mission, recording the nomadic tribes of the desert. Hani would help. He said it was easy. Just slaughter some goats and have a party.

Wherever I went, I had my recording equipment with me. I even brought it into the bathroom and set it in a corner when I took a shower. At bars I had it wrapped around my foot. Without it, I was just a tourist. Fresh batteries and microphone, tape, mike lines, flashlight and stands, all strapped together for security. The Nagra and the recording kit were heavy, about 50 or 60 pounds. After a recording safari, I would walk with one shoulder lower than the other for weeks.

> 1979

Sony brings out its Walkman, and cassettes soon replace LPs for the listening public.

The idea was to prepare a feast, tell the locals to come, and hope a passing caravan would stop at the sight of this grand gathering. I thought this was wishing for a lot but went along with his enthusiasm. We spent the next day getting ready. At the local market, I bought enough to feed 50 people. Hani prepared the goats with spices and herbs, and his housekeeper made a huge spit. By the late afternoon the meat was cooking, and the strong aroma was irresistible. The breeze on the desert took it out in all directions, where it signaled "come to my party, come to my tent, eat, drink, smoke, play music all night." Soon the horses and camels were parked everywhere. Guns were firing, horses were racing around the house—the party was on.

That afternoon I had positioned my two microphones carefully, one in some bushes and one in a tree that overhung the party area. Hani had a small porch where I stationed the Nagra. The mike lines were buried in the sand, carefully positioned to protect them from damage. Batteries were charged, tape was ready. Let the fireworks begin.

For two or three hours massive amounts of food were consumed. Hani then approached the musicians in the party, asking if they would play some music for my recording. They huddled off to the side and haggled among themselves over the price they wanted for their performance. They yelled and screamed, they laughed and patted each other on the back, as if they were about to close a major deal. Finally, they approached Hani with their offer: three hundred dollars for the night. This was big money for them. I doubled it, as was my custom in these situations. I knew the money meant a lot to them,

Mickey and the Dead's longtime promoter, Bill Graham, ride Arabians into the Egyptian desert after the band's performances at the pyramids. Their guide, Omar, had heard one of the concerts and told Mickey that the Dead's music made him feel "like that man on TV who leaps tall buildings and breaks bricks."

and I wanted them to give the music their all. (Later in my recording life I learned that a better approach is to let the local host, Hani in this case, handle the negotiations. Then, after the trip, follow up by sending photographs, copies of tapes, and any profits from a CD to the musicians or to a local cultural institution.)

First, that night, we all had to smoke. The guests formed a circle in the desert, and I was invited to smoke with them; actually, they insisted. This was part of the bargain. If I could still stand after the smoking, I would be allowed to record their music. I saw this as a test. Was I worthy of their sound? I accepted their challenge; this was not, after all, my first all-night smokeout. I was prepared to fly high to get the music flowing. The Bedouin were about to teach me just how tough field recording can be.

Hubble-bubbles were passed around the circle, refueled constantly by youngsters who stuffed them with huge amounts of hashish so strong that it had been mixed with tobacco as a stimulant to keep us from nodding off. This was "finger hash"—long fingerlike sticks of Moroccan Gold Seal hash. It looked like gold bullion from Fort Knox, with an official seal on each bundle stamped in gold. The kids efficiently crunched it up and loaded it in the pipe. The hubble-bubbles were passed around and around, the social chatter rising and falling.

What they said I do not know, but I could see them watching me from the corners of their eyes. "When would the stranger fall out, when would he throw up?" they were thinking. This was becoming an ordeal—the hash was great but I didn't smoke tobacco, so I was soon feeling sick. I held it in, fighting increasing nausea. *Can I last,* I wondered? I seemed to sit cross-legged in that circle for an eternity. Finally, it was time. They put down the pipes and said, "Let the music begin."

My Egyptian hosts seemed to relish this ritual of preparation, and I was stunned at the heroic amounts of hash that they could consume. I tried to get up, but my legs didn't respond to my brain. *Oh, my God,* I thought, *I can't walk.* What to do? The Nagra was a good 50 feet away. It was sitting there on the porch beckoning to me, but with the way I felt, it could have been on some far-off shore. All I could think was that the music was about to start and I was unarmed. I almost started to cry. Then it occurred to me—crawl. Crawl on your hands and knees.

As I crawled, I could taste the sand in my teeth. I pulled myself along like a soldier in battle, slowly, first the right elbow, then the left. Slowly I made my way to the steps of the porch. Four steps up—*oh no, this is going to be trouble*. I felt nothing; I just pulled my body along. Finally, the Nagra was in reach. Fortunately, I had loaded a reel of tape earlier in the day. All I had to do now was to turn the switch and it would be in record mode. I reached for the switch and to my horror there was no feeling in my fingers—my hand wouldn't work. This was bad. I almost started to cry. Hani was nowhere in sight and the music was about to begin. I lunged at the machine with my teeth and turned the switch to record. Then I propped myself in the corner as the first sounds started. Tape was rolling. I managed a laugh and a sigh of

Considered the ancestors of all Arabs and the true bearers of traditional Arab culture, the Bedouin have wandered the Sahara and Arabian deserts for countless centuries. Their love of poetry and music is legendary, leading some, like the man above, to fashion their own instruments.

relief. I knew they were watching me, but I didn't care. I finally had that machine working.

After about 30 minutes I regained control of my hands and feet. As the first reel came to an end, I replaced the tape and the night wore on. The party scene turned into a desert ritual. Horses circling, music wailing, drinking, smoking, and eating into the night. The musicians played for hours. I kept changing tape until the backup batteries gave out. And then so did I.

I remember nothing more until I woke up at dawn propped in the corner of a bedroom, the Nagra at my side, still set to record but now at a dead stop. A large bed was in the room, but somehow I had never found it and had slept on the floor. Walking outside in the sunlight, I saw that the desert was empty except for some debris, proof of the night's revelry. Hani was gone. I left a thank-you note for him and headed back to Cairo. With tapes in hand and memories of the last night fresh in my mind, I finally crawled into bed for a proper rest.

The next day the whole city of Cairo was buzzing with excitement. In Camp David, Maryland, Anwar Sadat had signed a peace accord with Israel, and he was returning home to a hero's welcome. What an opportunity! I grabbed my Nagra and went downtown to record the great city in full voice. Horns were blaring, people were screaming with joy, and the city was erupting with raw emotion. I climbed to a vantage point on the rooftop of a building to get a better recording. What a sound! I rolled tape as the city exploded. It was a fitting end to an incredible month of recording. I was ready to go home.

I ALWAYS HAD MY ANTENNA SCANNING FOR NEW SOUNDS, for music coming out of different traditions, music that broke the sound barrier for me. Around 1970, one of these new sounds came to me by way of an unmarked cassette, recorded from a public radio station by Robert Hunter, the lyricist for the Grateful Dead. It contained the chanting of Tibetan monks. That's all I knew. Their multiphonic vocalizing stunned me. Each monk had the ability to sing three notes simultaneously, something that was unheard of here in the West. At that time I had no way of finding out more about this unmarked tape.

Then, in 1972, I stumbled upon a recording of the Gyuto Tantric Choir's chants. Prof. Huston Smith's liner notes told their story: These Tibetan monks, whose spiritual leader was the Dalai Lama, had been living in exile in India since 1959. In that year, China invaded Tibet, razed their temples, and killed thousands of Tibetans, massacring them in the streets just for their spiritual beliefs and their land. The Tibetans didn't fight back, because they don't believe in violence. They kept practicing their brand of Buddhism, which has been around for more than 2,000 years. I knew some day I would run into the monks and record their strange but wonderful chants.

In 1985, Robert Thurman, one of the leading Tibetan scholars in America, brought the monks to the U.S. under the auspices of the Buddhist Society of America. While I was on tour with the Grateful Dead, word reached me that the monks were in the area. The next day I packed up my Nagra and headed to Amherst, Massachusetts, where I found the monks chanting in the Amherst College concert hall. I sat there smiling till my face hurt. Here they were.

Sublime chanting of the Gyuto Monks Tantric Choir echoes across the landscape at Mono Lake, California. Huston Smith, noted scholar of world religions, was the first to bring the monks' music to the attention of the Western world.

I tried to maintain my composure and be calm, but my heart raced. I introduced myself, and they asked me to join them for tea. All I could think of was rolling tape. How was I going to manage this? I wondered. It turned out that they were delightful, laughing and full of joy, happy to let me record their chants. The Dalai Lama believes that if even one ear and one heart are touched by these sacred sounds, the world will be a safer and more compassionate place.

They chanted, and I rolled tape for two hours or more, as the hair on my arms stood straight on end. I thought that not many people would hear their sounds, because the monks had no PA system and were chanting for audiences of just 20 or 30 people. It would take a thousand years to turn the world on at this pace. *I must bring them to the West Coast*, I thought. I had to ask them to come to S.F. and chant—chant for all my friends who just might understand their message of hope. The monks accepted my invitation. *Wait till Garcia hears this live*, I thought. *He's going to go bonkers, he'll love it*. Of course, to some of my friends these chants sounded like caged gorillas, as the superlow utterances can rattle your bones.

I arranged for a press conference to announce the show at the Berkeley Community Theater and to describe how the monks have the ability to chant three notes simultaneously. We all met on the steps in front of this great theater. I began my presentation, and I could see that the press people were writing on their pads, but their eyes were glazing over. Were they taking this seriously? To them, it must have seemed exotic, strange—and very San Francisco.

The concert was a smash hit, full house, great reviews. Now the sky was the limit. I could see the headlines, "Gyuto Monks on Tour." But first they needed a world-class recording to announce their presence, a sonic calling card. A big room was needed. A very big room.

That's where George Lucas came in—and his Skywalker Ranch. Two years later the Grateful Dead arranged for producing the next tour.

[ABOVE] Mickey Hart prepares the Gyuto Monks for a performance in 1995. Mickey has produced several albums of the Tantric choir's chants. As the liner notes to the *Perfect Jewel* album explain, their chanting "emanates from samadhi ('a trancelike state of pure consciousness') and is capable of communicating that samadhi to the listener...." Not entertainment but prayer, the chants "are thought to arise only from the throat of a person who has realized selfless wisdom."

[OPPOSITE] The monks perform in traditional saffron dress.

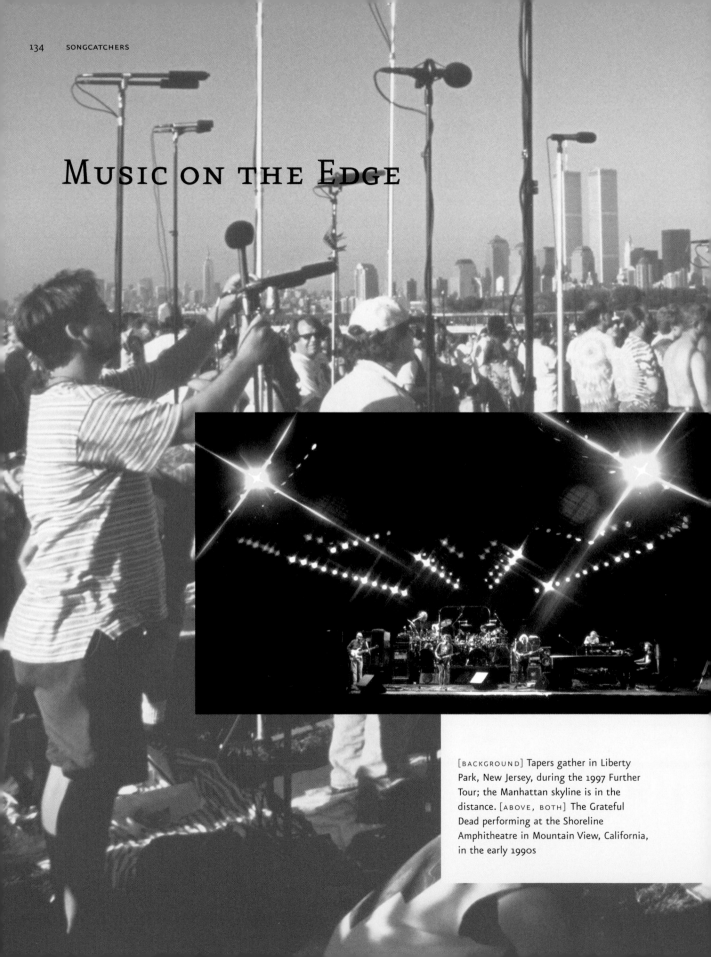

MUSIC ON THE EDGE

[BACKGROUND] Tapers gather in Liberty Park, New Jersey, during the 1997 Further Tour; the Manhattan skyline is in the distance. [ABOVE, BOTH] The Grateful Dead performing at the Shoreline Amphitheatre in Mountain View, California, in the early 1990s

"I wanted to hear a three-dimensional drum sound with each and every component clear and distinct. I wanted 'space' around each instrument and voice. I wanted the vocals to caress the audience. I made my recordings of the band simply as a way of keeping a record of my mixes, a sort of diary or sonic journal."

—*Owsley Stanley*

Technology has always been a part of how the Grateful Dead made their music. In their early days in Haight Ashbury, they had the help of a pioneering technical wizard—known in band lore as Owsley or Bear— to provide PA quality then almost unknown. With rock music a relatively new phenomenon, the technology to handle its sound effectively and project it was still lacking. But Owsley, along with another wizard named John Meyer, developed a PA system that would change everything. And he began recording the band's live performances.

The ambience of the sound space was particularly important because the Grateful Dead was not simply a proscenium band. It was an interactive experience. For some people, that interaction included making audience tapes of the shows. Known as "tapers," these people started off as a small group in the early '70s and

eventually became a culture unto themselves. With the tapers, field recording expanded beyond scholars or adventuresome hobbyists and became part of the popular culture.

The intrinsic power of live music exists in the moment. For the musician, the mission is in the discovery and habitation of the sound at that particular fraction of time. For the taper, the preservation of the Grateful Dead's music on tape became a way to reinhabit that moment. As Jerry Garcia put it, "Once we're done with it [the music], the tapers can have it." In its purest form, a recording can stream the listener into the flow of time, effortlessly and with heightened awareness, just as a smell can reawaken memories. "When I listen to one of my tapes, I can remember what I was doing when I made it, who I was sitting beside, what the lights were like during a particular song. I re-enter

that moment," says David Lemieux, a former taper who is now the Grateful Dead's audiovisual archivist. "As much as simply the experience of the music, the tapers were into the thrill of the chase, to capture the moment live. And to be at a concert when the Dead played that particular song you'd been waiting and waiting to get on tape."

Music on the edge deserved cutting-edge technology, and the tapers taught each other about innovations in audio engineering and information technology. Rapid miniaturization and the increased ease of use of recording devices, as well as more affordable prices, led to an explosion of the taper culture. And as early as 1974, some of the more technoid tapers gathered in Stanford's Artificial Intelligence Lab (SAIL) and used set lists from Dead concerts as the elements of the kind of

database technology that still drives e-commerce today.

Taping was a ritual of community. At its most elemental, the social architecture of the taping culture was based on the simple human desire to share and transmit knowledge—the same instinct that has driven most field recordists to record. Each taper was an archivist in his or her own right, and most were anxious to swap tapes and information with each other. In 1999, that music-sharing philosophy went global with the advent of Napster. Through a technology known as peer-to-peer computing, Napster allowed music to be passed around through easy, on-line file sharing.

This sent shock waves through the music industry, which saw its control of distribution channels threatened. The record companies viewed the

exchange of music as stealing and a violation of copyright, and an intense round of lobbying and legal action began. In 1998 the Digital Millennium Copyright Act (DCMA) was passed by Congress, extending copyrights for the life of an artist plus 70 years; copyrights owned by corporations run for 95 years. Napster is no longer, but the urge to share music is alive and well, and other file-sharing services have sprung up in its stead.

We record to preserve access, the access that music has always been about, the transportation to "other times forgotten space." It would be a betrayal of the spirit, a failure of the role of the artist, not to attempt to maximize that access. No doubt future "soundcatchers" will use science to explore our musical past and enable our musical future.

ELIZABETH COHEN
Stanford University

[OPPOSITE] To open the Gyuto Tantric Choir's 1988 tour, Mickey, Philip Glass, and Kitaro performed at St. John the Divine in New York.

[BACKGROUND] The Oakland Coliseum is filled for a Grateful Dead New Year's Eve concert in 1988. The enormous PA system is visible on the far right.

Lucas told me he had a very big, state-of-the-art room that would be perfect. It was modeled after a room at IRCAM, a national institute in France devoted to cutting-edge audio research and music. The walls and ceiling had mechanized panels that could be easily moved and adjusted, changing the acoustic properties at will. A large, bright room could be made into a nonreverberant space in a matter of minutes. You could tune the room to the music's needs in an instant. *What a marvel*, I thought. When I walked in for the first time, my breath left me for a moment. It was the grandest of spaces, huge beyond belief. It reminded me of studios from the golden era of the '40s, the ones in which large orchestras played scores for romantic movies. The monks would sound amazing here. I made the calls, first to Tom Flye, my sound engineer. "Get a recording truck with the best equipment, bring it to Skywalker Ranch tomorrow, and let's record the monks multitrack."

Tom rented a 32-track digital recorder and 32 super-high-quality pre-amps. We plugged the pre-amps into the tape machine, which gave us the cleanest of signals. We begged and borrowed the finest micro-phones in the land, and recording began in earnest.

The monks were amazed at the first sight of the Skywalker soundstage. It was world class. George had vision and he had money. This was a testament to both.

The room soon filled up with the sound of monks chanting. I sat behind the console and smiled. Here in the land of silver screen myths, laser beams, and Yoda, the monks were singing an ancient music. George came to the sessions, soaked up the sound, and reveled in the way his new room was performing. Along with George was his chief of staff, the no-nonsense but kindly Jane Bay. Jane hung around the sessions long after George retreated to his office complex. I didn't notice at the time, but the monks were working their magic on her. She eased back in her chair and the sound coming out of the speakers grabbed her soul and moved her deeply. "The sound resonated at the depth of my being.... To me it sounded like the pulse of the universe," she wrote years later in her book, *Precious Jewels of Tibet*. Jane is now a practicing Buddhist and has made pilgrimages to Tibet. The monks won her, heart and soul.

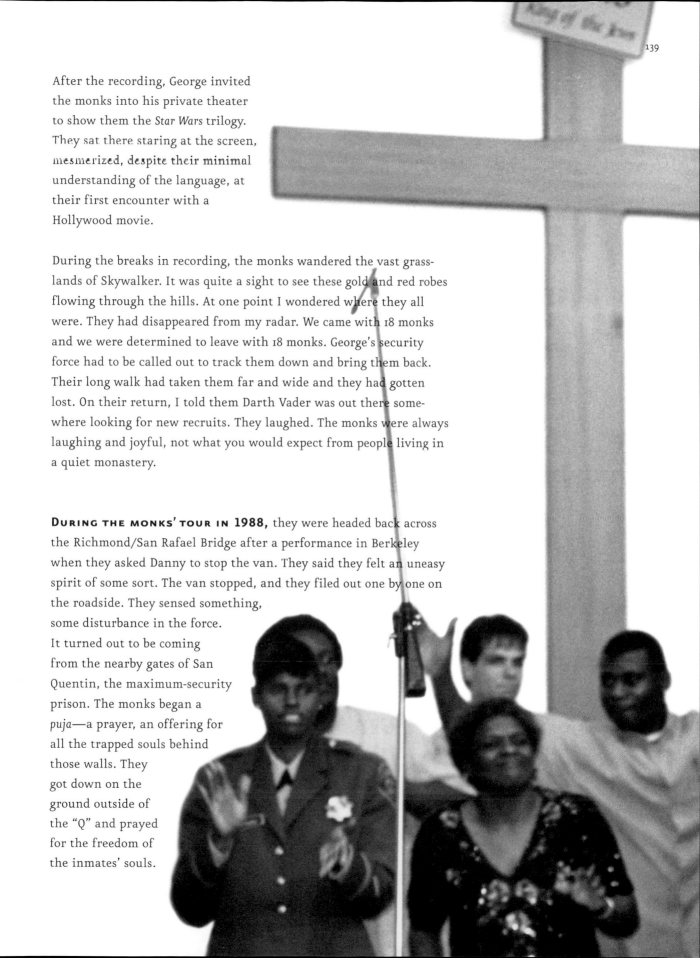

After the recording, George invited
the monks into his private theater
to show them the *Star Wars* trilogy.
They sat there staring at the screen,
mesmerized, despite their minimal
understanding of the language, at
their first encounter with a
Hollywood movie.

During the breaks in recording, the monks wandered the vast grass-
lands of Skywalker. It was quite a sight to see these gold and red robes
flowing through the hills. At one point I wondered where they all
were. They had disappeared from my radar. We came with 18 monks
and we were determined to leave with 18 monks. George's security
force had to be called out to track them down and bring them back.
Their long walk had taken them far and wide and they had gotten
lost. On their return, I told them Darth Vader was out there somewhere looking for new recruits. They laughed. The monks were always
laughing and joyful, not what you would expect from people living in
a quiet monastery.

DURING THE MONKS' TOUR IN 1988, they were headed back across
the Richmond/San Rafael Bridge after a performance in Berkeley
when they asked Danny to stop the van. They said they felt an uneasy
spirit of some sort. The van stopped, and they filed out one by one on
the roadside. They sensed something,
some disturbance in the force.
It turned out to be coming
from the nearby gates of San
Quentin, the maximum-security
prison. The monks began a
puja—a prayer, an offering for
all the trapped souls behind
those walls. They
got down on the
ground outside of
the "Q" and prayed
for the freedom of
the inmates' souls.

When the monks returned to the U.S. three years
later, they asked for and were granted permission to
enter the prison. They had heard there was a gospel
choir behind the walls and wanted to exchange good
feelings with them. The San Quentin gospel choir
was told they'd have some unusual visitors. They
weren't sure about that. Would these guys in robes
try to convert them away from Jesus? Would
Jesus approve of a visit from these Buddhists? The choir talked
about it with their chaplain and in the end they decided that,
since "the Lord works in mysterious ways," maybe this
was one of those times. It certainly was. The monks and
the gospel choir spent an evening singing, praying,
and chanting together.

Through this visit the Gyuto monks did more than bless me with their music. They put me in touch with a completely different brand of spiritual sound. This was to become one of the strangest, most difficult, and most satisfying recording experiences of my life.

Danny Rifkin, a former business manager of the Grateful Dead, was now head of the Grateful Dead-sponsored Society of Gyuto Sacred Arts. He was leading the monks' tour and accompanied them into the prison. Danny was impressed with the enthusiasm of the San Quentin choir. He came up with the idea that I should record the prisoners' gospel singing. I agreed to go to a Sunday service and check them out. After a tight security check, we entered through the main gates. This was scary stuff.

The Reverend Earl Smith—a burly man, now a straight-up minister— was in charge of the choir. He knew all the games that are played out behind the walls. He was kind and strong, just what's needed on the inside. He welcomed us with a curious eye. He couldn't believe we wanted to come inside, record the choir, pay all costs of recording (with the help of the Rex Foundation, the Grateful Dead's charitable arm), and wanted nothing in return. But he didn't know Danny's zeal for the good. Danny just wanted some love to be spread around.

The music itself was under the direction of Mandell Motley. Motley turned out to be the sweetest guy you ever wanted to meet. He knew harmony and melody and was doing 20 years for interstate bad checks. Totally nonviolent, Motley was on the Lord's side. The choir and band really cooked that day; they had this sense of real prayer. They were here praying for salvation. This wasn't some church in the suburbs, it was the Q. There were no guns allowed in the chapel, but as soon as you walked out into the yard, watch out. They were fully loaded and just aimed for trouble. The catwalks were full of the ominous faces of guards, men and women who would just as easily fit the description of special forces operatives. It wasn't pretty. I tried not to look.

But the songs. The songs were full of salvation and freedom, words of love and Jesus, long lonely nights, atonement of past sins. This was for real. They would testify, "When I first came to San Quentin and that steel door slammed shut, I dropped to my knees and cried, cried to you, 'Oh, Lord, please help me, help me make it through the night.' And you came to me Jesus, thank you lord." I felt the spirit; you could

[OPPOSITE] Lead singer Ron Williams and the members of the San Quentin choir bring their energetic faith to the recordings on their album, *He's All I Need*. Even as Hart prepared the choir for recording sessions, riots erupted in Los Angeles and an inmate on death row was executed. But singer Williams's faith remained unshaken. He had always wanted to sing professionally, he said. "I had given up hope, but now, through God's grace, it's come true. Here I am in prison, and I found joy and peace."

cut it with a knife. *Could I really do this?* Their singing was ragtag in many ways, and microphones have no mercy. I would have to work them hard to bring them up to professional standards. *Would they take direction?* Reverend Smith talked to them after I left, and they agreed to go for it. The warden, Daniel Vasquez, gave permission for the recording to happen.

I spent weeks going into San Quentin to rehearse the choir. Reverend Smith assigned me an inmate to accompany me everywhere. His name was Donald Cronk. He was the only guilty person I ran into behind those walls. (Everyone else swore he was innocent.) When he was 24 with a drug problem, Cronk had killed a man during a robbery gone bad. He admitted it, and today he says that if there were anything he could do for the murdered man's family, "I would gladly do it in a token effort to try and repay the horrible nightmares that they have had to live with." I liked Cronk. He was a gentle guy with the sharpest mind. At the end of each day he would meet me at the first gate and hand me computer readouts of everything I said that day. He was flawless, the best assistant I ever had. Cronk and I became friends during those months, and I have written his parole board many times in his favor, but he will never see the walls from the other side.

At first the choir was all male, but slowly the sound of the rehearsals reached the ears of female guards and office workers, who joined in. It was quite a sight to see some of the tiny female guards holding hands with these huge inmates, eyes shut, swaying back and forth in deep prayer. "Does this happen all the time here?" I inquired. "Not really, Mickey," Earl told me. This was a first and a big deal, getting approval for the female guards to sing with the male inmates. Things were happening so fast I didn't ask too many questions. The whole thing became a kind of healing event; music can have that effect. And everybody involved gave up a lot to do the rehearsals— the guards gave up personal time with their families, and the prisoners missed sleep, "yard time," visits from friends and loved ones, sometimes even meals.

Finally, the day of the recording arrived. Although everyone was excited, the whole prison was on edge. For the first time in 25 years, a prison execution had taken place, and everyone was worked up. Still, 18 days after the execution, we began recording *He's All I Need*.

> 1982-83

Compact discs and players are marketed worldwide.

The guards were especially cranky as the giant recording truck was wheeled into the main yard and positioned. Some of the guards loved this project because it relieved tension and calmed the whole inmate population. The others hated it, since they thought any good thing that happened to the inmates was a form of coddling

Tom Flye was in the chief engineers' seat in the truck. Tom never blinked; he just rolled tape. We had a visual hookup into the chapel from the truck in the main yard. The inmates had made a huge banner that hung on the wall, renaming the chapel "Studio Q." They were really into this by now. Packing blankets lined the walls. We had transformed the chapel into a sound garden, and what a sight it was. Still, I often thought, *I just hope I make it out of here alive today.* This was no cakewalk.

We rolled tape all day, recording the basic tracks without the lead vocals. Then we doubled the track with the vocalists singing on top of the previous tracks.

Near the end of the sessions, I had a special treat for the choir. I brought in Kentucky Fried Chicken, but this was not smart. Apparently, mealtimes are among the most dangerous moments in prisons. Most fights and arguments occur when blood sugar is low. So, before our meal, with the smell of KFC wafting through the chapel, a choir member was slipped a chicken wing by the librarian, who was guarding it at the back of the chapel. The others saw this, and the war was on. In prison, the inmates are acutely aware of what others are getting, and wondering why they don't have it, too.

A lovely blonde guard by the name of Angel was standing next to me. She had been singing with the choir for months. She was also their jailer. No guns on her in here, though. I turned to Angel and asked what to do. She shot back the order to "Hold the line." So I did: No eating until we finish the session. At that moment one inmate lost control and dashed to the chapel door that led out into the main yard. Now a person running into that night is at grave risk. The guards just shoot. You do not run out there. You walk slowly during the day and night. Every 20 feet you must stop and get verbal and sight recognition from the guards on the catwalk. As the inmate ran toward the door, my heart started to race. He put his shoulder to it, and it flew open. Everyone stopped breathing for a moment. Just as he lunged toward the main yard, the long strong arm of another inmate grabbed him by the collar and reeled him in. We stood around him and calmed him down. That was a close one, but we managed to finish the recording without fatalities.

After a week or two we arranged to have our main soloists overdub their parts at Fantasy Studios in Berkeley. Earl had talked the warden into it, but the arrangements were far from simple. When the truck arrived at the studios, the guards got out first and looked around. This whole situation was highly unusual, not only for the guards but also for the staff at Fantasy. Roy Seigel, the studio boss, had graciously given us a marvelous room for the day. It was a Sunday, the holy day, a great day to roll tape. The guards secured the entrance and exit doors to the studio. Guns were cocked and ready. The guards brought the soloists in and positioned them in the main record room. I immediately noticed that they were shackled and in cuffs. Over the last few months, we had become friends and I just couldn't record them in irons. I begged the guards to uncuff them and let them sing without restraints. The guards felt the spirit of the moment and reluctantly obliged. The session went down without a hitch, and the singers were taken back to the Q that night as promised.

We faced one last obstacle. Our main lead singer on one song was a murderer and the warden just wouldn't allow him outside the walls. He used headphones to hear the choir on the first machine as we recorded his voice on the second. QTV covered our whole recording process in the chapel, so the inmate population could see what was going on.

On the liner notes to the album, the choir says:

> "We cannot help but feel that the spirit of the Lord is upon us now more than ever…. This is not an ending of the paths of diverse and adverse people, but the source of a message; that there are no barriers to realizing the glory of God."

This is what the Gyuto Tantric monks believe about their music, too.

In the end, the San Quentin album, *He's All I Need*, climbed the billboard charts and nestled comfortably in the top 25 in the country. Quite an accomplishment.

> **1987**

Digital Audio Tape (DAT) players are introduced.

Aside from the power of the music itself, the Gyuto recordings and the San Quentin album were successful because they benefited from the latest technology—a technology that caught the nuances and spiritual energy behind the sound in ways that a two-track tape could never do. These tapes were a far cry from my field recordings of the Bedouin, but I was soon to find out that field recordings, too, could become works of art with the help of this new technology.

I WAS IN THE MIDDLE OF RESEARCH that would become *Drumming at the Edge of Magic* and *Planet Drum* when I first met Professor Steven Feld. I was looking for the link between rhythm, trance, and ritual. My partner Fred Lieberman was on the scholarly side of our relationship and knew the tribe of ethnos well. He suggested that I call a fellow ethnomusicologist who does groundbreaking work in the New Guinea rain forests. "He is one of us," Fred said.

Daibo Tulunei, a young Kaluli drummer, tunes his lizard-skin drumhead by adjusting its arrangement of beeswax bumps. He and ten other drummers played for 12 continuous hours to celebrate the arrival of the Kaluli dictionary produced by Steven Feld.

One day in 1984, I called Feld. "You don't know me, I'm a drummer in a rock-and-roll band, but a friend of mine told me you know about music in New Guinea, and I wanted to know if we could get together and talk about it." He said, "Sure, come on over."

I went to his house the morning after a show, and I remember his soft voice. I kept inching my chair closer and closer to hear him, saying, "You gotta speak up. Remember, I'm a drummer in a rock-and-roll band." He was young and intense and looked to me like Dustin Hoffman. His Philadelphia apartment was lined with all things New Guinea. In front of his fireplace stood a piglike creature made of bamboo or rattan. Boars' teeth and bird feathers could be seen around the room. *This guy was the real deal*, I thought.

Steven Feld had made an aural tapestry of a day in the life of the rain forest. What an amazing revelation. The sounds of the rain, the crickets, the cicadas, the birds, all entwining with the beautiful voices of these spiritual people. This, I thought, was a masterwork.

"I'm interested in drums and trance," I told him. "Do you know any origin myths, legends, stories? Can you describe the experience of being in the rain forest?" Meeting him, I had hit the mother lode, and I couldn't get the questions out of my mouth quickly enough. Here was a living, breathing treasure trove of information, not a book written in scholarese by some white man. He not only spoke the language of the Kaluli rain forest people, but he was compiling and editing the first Kaluli dictionary.

He began by telling me of his experiences with the Kaluli people, who live in the Bosavi region of the Papua New Guinea highlands. He described the way that a Bosavi drum takes on the voice of a bird. When the Kaluli make a drum, they capture a certain bird—the Papuan bellbird—and put its syrinx, or voice box, in the drum, so that the instrument becomes the pulsing voice of the bird. I was intoxicated by our conversation.

I asked him how he got such close-up recordings of these birds. He told me that sometimes he would have to sit in the trees all night to capture the cycle of nature. Are there snakes? "Of course," he said, "small and deadly." I could never, ever imagine myself sitting in the middle of a New Guinea rain forest in the dead of night with my Nagra, while snakes—the death adder, in particular—were crawling around. Their poison could kill you in about ten minutes, unless of course you had your handy antivenin neatly frozen by your side.

Feld was a real remote recordist on the edge. I was mightily impressed.

He told me he had just made a recording for National Public Radio called *Voices in the Forest*. It condensed 24 hours in the rain forest to a half hour. He then played it for me. "That's amazing, I can't believe it's such a secret." "It's not a secret," he said.

"Please, give me this tape, and come to the Dead show tonight at the Spectrum. At intermission, we're going to put this thing on, and we'll have

Deep in the rain forest of Papua New Guinea, Bosavi teacher and guide Yubi scans the canopy for birds, while Steven Feld stands by with a parabolic microphone and Nagra, waiting to record.

[OPPOSITE] At an all-night ceremony, Feld records Ilailo, a singer, and other Bosavi musicians. The recordings from his 1982 trip were broadcast in Papua New Guinea on Feld's radio program, *Voices in the Forest*.

20,000 Dead Heads turn into tree-climbing monkeys. You're not going to believe it."

Steven sat on the stage right behind me when the tape started playing. People in the audience were loving it, whistling to it. They became the rain forest, responding to the animals, mimicking them, and answering their calls. What fun. I could see Steven's face; he later told me he was thinking, "Oh no, what am I getting into? Do I want all these people 'grooving' to the music of the Kaluli?" But then he realized that was an elitist reaction. I told him that if I loved the music, there were probably thousands of people out there who would, too. "I'd love to work with you on this kind of thing, really get it out to the public the right way, using the best technology," I told Feld. "Call me when you're ready to take the next step."

Jerry Garcia (standing) joins Mickey and his sound engineer Tom Flye (far left) in the Skywalker studio during a recording session of the Dzintar Latvian Women's Choir.

In 1990, Feld told me he was headed to New Guinea on his annual trek. "Are you interested in doing a CD of *Voices in the Forest?*" I asked. If so, I wanted it to be state of the art this time. The plan was to equip Feld not just with the Nagra, but a Nagra on steroids. It would be strapped in a new way. The new Bryston Dolby SR noise reduction unit was designed to be attached directly to the bottom of the Nagra. New superclean microphone pre-amps were added and LED meters measured the quietest of sounds, like a microscope for audio. Now the floor of the rain forest would come into perfect focus. The Nagra would be able to register sounds that until now only the human ear could perceive and process. The batteries would have solar-powered recharging capabilities, and parabolic reflectors and shotgun mikes would be able to home in on distant birds and critters. This was something that had never been attempted in the field before, let alone in a rain forest.

Feld is a remarkable person. He started out thinking of himself as a jazz musician. In college he read books about the blues and jazz that made him understand the connection between race and music. In the spring of 1968, when Martin Luther King, Jr., was killed, Feld was very involved in antiwar activities. He wanted to study music and think about music in ways that went beyond just being a musician, that would help illuminate the link between racism and militarism. He decided to change his major to anthropology and met anthropologist Colin Turnbull. Turnbull asked Feld to help analyze and understand some of the Pygmy music he had recorded. Feld realized he could do something with music that was cultural, political, and musical. Through music, he could imagine alternate ways of being a person in the world.

Feld found his connection to Africa through jazz and went to graduate school at Indiana University, where he studied with the famous ethnomusicologist Alan Merriam. Indiana also had a world-class African Studies program. The young Feld planned to do fieldwork in Africa. But in 1972, he heard Bosavi music from Papua New Guinea for the first time, and it stunned him. Through their cosmology, through their compositional history, through 40,000 years of their evolution in the rain forest, the Bosavi had linked birdsong and music. And they cried in response to their ceremonial music. That was their aesthetic, their way of participating in the ceremony. Feld had never heard anything like it in the world. It was incredible.

Feld recorded it but couldn't figure out who would put out recordings of birdcalls and crying. The academic community wasn't interested in this, though some musicians and people on the cutting edge of music were. So Feld's work was largely ignored. He couldn't get a job in anthropology or ethnomusicology, because what he was doing was too offbeat, so he got a job instead teaching film at the University of Pennsylvania, in the Annenberg School of Communications in the early 1980s, when we first met.

Once I had Feld outfitted with the best technology imaginable, he went back to Papua New Guinea for a long summer in 1990, recording about 22 hours in the rain forest. When he came back, he used my studio to put it all together and produce *Voices of the Rainforest*.

> **1999**

Shawn Fanning, a student at Northwestern University, develops the file-sharing software that gives birth to Napster.

A tropical rain forest is teeming with life. It's loud—very loud—with all the sounds running together in nature's marvelous cacophony. The challenge has always been to record the delicate details that make up this wall of sound. Feld calls the phenomenon "lift-up-over-sounding." As one wave of sound recedes, the next one comes forward, taking its place. The sea of sound, be it rain, insects, wind, or animals, never ends. The thought was to record the height and depth of the rain forest's sounds in stereo layers, from the gentle stereo surround of ambient sounds to the specific directional sounds of voices and instruments. These soundscape layers could then be woven together on a multitrack machine back in my studio. The environment would be mixed in its natural lift-up-over-sounding way, and the recordings would weave together the rhythm of the day to make a living sound tapestry.

When we were making the recordings, my wife Caryl figured out how to get the royalties from the Bosavi music back to the rain forest people themselves. Through the Tides Foundation in San Francisco we set up the Bosavi People's Fund, which helps the Bosavi protect their land from multinational logging and other interests.

Feld says my style is a kind of musical activism, the object being to get the work of field recordists out to the public.

On Earth Day, 1991, we invited members of the music industry to a release party for *Voices of the Rainforest* at Skywalker Ranch. We showed slides of the rain forest and explained that the recording was all about rain forests, about the people who live in them, about how their lives and their music could be endangered by the incursion of extractive resource companies. Then we held another release party for the press in San Francisco.

For Feld, who came from academia, this was all a very new experience. The Bosavi became the beneficiaries of my connections. Don Rose, the president of Rykodisc, was a visionary. He and his partner Arthur Mann put their hearts and souls into this project. I could now walk up to the head of Tower Records and say, "Look, you need to have a bin for Papua New Guinea where you can put this music. It shouldn't be under 'Mickey Hart,' or 'Pacific.'"

All music deserves to be recorded as well as Grateful Dead music is recorded. Two thousand people in the middle of a rain forest should have the benefit of the same equipment, the same studios, and the same distribution system. I told this to all who would listen. This was all about discovering the world, but it was also about respect for other music and musicians.

Feld got thousands of letters from Dead Heads and others, and he realized the dream of reaching an audience far beyond academia. Through the music—through the sounds of these people singing about, for, and with the birds—he was able to reach people far beyond the limited audience of ethnomusicologists, rain forest activists, and anthropologists.

Mickey, on a Bombo Indio drum, beats out the rhythm for a masked Flora Purim and Airto Moreira. Husband and wife, the two musicians were part of Mickey's *Planet Drum* experiment, in which percussionists from different musical traditions came together to speak the universal language of rhythm. The experiment—and the resulting album—were both successes.

epilogue

Quiet energy surrounds you as you enter the main reading room at the Library of Congress. Columns of marble rise up to the vaulted ceiling like the legs of some giant creature. Massive bronze and iron statues gaze down with knowing eyes. Among the library's holdings are millions of stories, tales, and legends. This is the Oz of libraries, the mother lode—530 miles of bookshelves lie in my path. The chase that will result in this book begins here, and my heart starts to pound. Where to go? Where to start? My senses are overwhelmed in this sea of knowledge. I have to focus and I choose Jesse Walter Fewkes. He is my direct ancestor, after all, the first American to make a field recording by mechanical means.

"Few structures represent human thought and aspiration in such dramatic fashion," one historian wrote of the Library of Congress. The library's main reading room soars 162 feet to a domed ceiling, with concentric circles of study desks for the scholars and researchers who have flocked here for more than a century.

What led me to this chase to begin with were the stories of Fewkes and the recordists who came after him. What was it like to be Jesse on that cold and windy day, March 15, 1890, in Calais, Maine? Did he know he was making history? How can I glide out into the field with him and feel what he felt when Noel Josephs started singing and the stylus started etching into that wax cylinder? Fewkes must have been amazed that Mr. Edison's newfangled talking machine even worked. But it did, and the result of those days in Calais is really what has sent me, over a hundred years later, to the Library of Congress.

In some ways, the library has been my home away from home for years. The path there led from my experiences as a field recordist to my more recent years as a sound preservationist. The preservation work started for me in 1985, when I got a call from Tony Seeger, grandson of the great musicologist Charles and nephew of the famous folksingers Pete, Mike, and Peggy Seeger. Tony is a musical hunter-gatherer extraordinaire who has done extensive fieldwork in the

Amazon. But at the time he called me, he had been thrust into a new world, that of preservation and the record business. He was to oversee the digital transfer of Smithsonian Folkways recordings purchased from the estate of Moe Asch, one of the great musical collections of all time. Tony knew very little about the digital revolution and the new machines and gizmos that were cropping up daily. But he knew I was directly involved in this new technology. He asked me to join the Board of Directors at Smithsonian Folkways and make sure that Moe's life-work would move into the digital domain at the highest level of quality available.

There was, as always, little money available for indigenous or folk music, so I had to rely once again on the good ol' Grateful Dead. Our mastering engineer, Joe Gastwirt, had the machines and the know-how to start this new venture off on the right foot. The challenge was to peel back the pops, clicks, and hisses inherent in early recording equipment without destroying the original source material. The crickets and dogs and coughing would not be touched, only the sonic debris left by technology. This was a delicate operation, very much like cleaning and restoring an old painting. Slowly and carefully, we sonically bathed these old masters and cleaned them up so the world could finally hear what was on them. My thought was that any recordists worth their salt would want the tapes to reflect the way the music sounded when they first heard it with their own ears.

After launching Leadbelly and Woody Guthrie anew, I moved on to the Folkways Navajo recordings made by Laura Boulton in the 1930s and '40s. Then the old kahuna chants from Hawaii. After a while we developed a systematic approach, and I didn't need to oversee the process personally anymore.

In 1990, Tom Vennum, senior ethnomusicologist at the Smithsonian, said, "Mickey, they really need your expertise at the Library of Congress." Dr. James Billington, the Librarian then and now, is a tall, gray-haired intellectual who specializes in all things Russian, including the glories of Russian bells. Billington was determined to digitize the Library of Congress—including its music.

Tom and I walked up the street to the Library of Congress's American Folklife Center. The director at the time was Alan Jabbour, a fine fiddle player who was caught up in the life of curating and overseeing the largest collection of indigenous music in the world. I spread my Rykodisc World Series recordings, all 20 or so, on the large wooden table in his office and told him "Your collection deserves to be preserved and presented like this." We decided to create the Endangered Music Project—a way to preserve the music of people from all over the Earth.

"Analogue—non-digital—recording degrades over time, and every time you make a copy, you lose quality. But if the sound is in binary form, it can be migrated to future generations of computers without losing any of its quality." —*Michael Taft, Head, Archive of Folk Culture, American Folklife Center*

The musics contained in the library's vast recordings would last only as long as the medium on which they were recorded. You have to preserve the physical object containing the recording, as well as the machines that can play it back, if you want to preserve the music. In the century since Edison recorded "Mary had a little lamb," we've been imprinting sound on tinfoil, wax, metal, wire, glass, acetate, vinyl, magnetic tape, and most recently, plastic. Each of these technologies has its own set of problems: Impurities in manufacture; innate poisons in the substances; decay, rot, and mold from exposure to air and improper storage conditions; and for tape, hiss, print-through, and "sticky shed syndrome." The death knell is sounding for early recordings. It's a race against time for the serious musical preservationist to transfer the contents from the original medium onto some newer, better one. Today, that means migrating it into the digital domain. Digitization is the safest technology so far for storage and playback, because once digitized the content can be moved automatically to new technologies without loss of quality. The digital domain also allows compact storage, a far cry from storing boxes of fragile wax cylinders or acetate disks.

In the case of wax cylinders, which have the oldest, rarest recordings, the wax is very fragile, and the cylinders can only be played a certain number of times before they're used up. The music is trapped on those cylinders. It's a Catch-22. If you play a cylinder, you're damaging it, shortening its life span. If you don't play it, it has no purpose. Since 1979, the Library of Congress has been busy with the Federal Cylinder Project, transferring the music into digital form.

It's a painstaking process. For starters, you have to worry about speed. It's easy to get the speed wrong. Sometimes you have to correct archival mistakes made in the past, such as the too-slow master tapes made from Frances Densmore's amazing collection of American Indian cylinders. Only now is that mistake being corrected.

Recordings have lives of their own. They can revitalize the cultures they came from, bring the music back to life, give people back their identity. Keeping musics alive through preservation allows them to be repatriated to the cultures that originally created them. And that goes some way toward balancing the ledgers for what was taken from these cultures during centuries of colonization, war, economic exploitation, and missionizing. In the 1970s Native Americans started asking for copies of music on wax-cylinder recordings so they could re-learn the chants and songs that had been lost over generations of mis-sionizing and re-education. Those recordings breathed new life into their present-day rituals and traditions.

In some ways, the old recordings can conjure the past to life. I've taken part in that process in several ways: as a recordist and a preservationist and as a percussionist for the Grateful Dead. Since the Dead Head tapers record every performance, I know our music will live forever, so I'm free to create a new version of the song every time I play it. As a jam band, that's what the Grateful Dead—now the Dead—is all about.

In the late 1990s, when we took a break from playing, our music went on through recordings, particularly the ones the tapers had made. They've created their own culture around our music, with their own rules. In some ways their rituals became stronger during the seven years we stopped performing. And in some ways, I think those rituals played a part in bringing us back together.

Music is an aural tradition, like language. And we know that languages are dying at an inconceivable rate: A language disappears from the planet every two weeks, when the last person who speaks it dies. When the language dies, so do the songs. Every musician is drawing to some extent on the musicians that came before him or her. For instance, when a musician begins to learn new skills on an instrument, she usually bases her knowledge on a body of earlier work. Eventually, she will create new musics out of the old. If there had been no Appalachian back-porch music, no Delta blues, no Woody Guthrie, perhaps there would be no Grateful Dead. Perhaps there would be no Carlos Santana or Paul Simon.

I truly believe there is no music left that has not been fused with some other tradition, except the musics that have been isolated behind monastery walls, like that of the Gyuto Tantric Monks or the music of people in extremely remote areas. Diasporas, trade routes, migrations dating back to the earliest human cultures have spread musical ideas across the globe. Now we have technologies, distribution systems,

"When I hear the cylinders, they lead to thoughts about what songs were still alive and what songs we had lost....We shall not be false to any great truths...if we listen to the olden voice, an unseen heritage of our bounteous land, as it sings of our unity with nature."

—Dennis Hastings, Omaha tribal archivist

The irreplacable music on the old Folkways label is slowly being digitized.

Working with Rykodisc, Mickey Hart produced The World, a series of digitally remastered field recordings for the Library of Congress's Endangered Music Project.

satellite transmission, and the world's music available at the press of a button. We don't even have to go to a record store anymore. We just dial up music in cyberspace or go to our digital radios and tune in the world.

Who owns music? Music is a personal creation, a performance, a skill developed over a period of time. It is also a possession, the intellectual property of the person who creates it. But like any commodity, it can be sold, traded, or given away. It comes out of the musician's mind and soul, but it is unheard until the musician picks up an instrument or sings a melody and transforms an idea into sound. That is what makes intellectual property tangible. Recorded sound freezes the music in time, makes it accessible forever. Recording gives physical representation to an intangible idea. Now a musician can leave a songprint, and copyright laws protect it.

"Ethnomusicologists preserve, memorialize, and mediate traditions.... The transmission of traditions is an old and deep aspect of [their] research process."

—Kay Shelemay, Chair, American Folklife Center

We must find creative ways to pay for the musics we have recorded in the field by funneling profits back into the cultures. If the original musicians or their kin cannot be located, we can fund local music schools or other cultural institutions. For instance, we returned all of the profits from the Gyuto Monks' recordings so that they could build a monastery and college in Dharamsala, India. These recordings help support the monks' life in exile. In the case of the Bosavi of New Guinea, we helped them protect their environment. Flora, fauna, environment are all related to culture. There is a grand weave to everything on this planet. If we want the Bosavi in New Guinea to keep

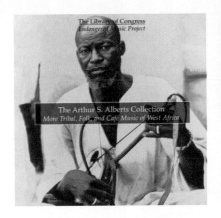

making their rain forest music, they've got to have the forest and its birds and other sounds around them to do that. Destroy their environment and the animals that live in it and you run the risk of destroying their culture and their music.

For preservationists, the race against time can never be won. The Endangered Music Project at the Library of Congress is now engaged in triage, trying to identify and digitize the most endangered of its recordings for preservation and commercial release—but some of the recordings won't make it. The library's staff for the Federal Cylinder Project also has been hard at work for decades, trying to copy the music from their wax cylinders onto a safer medium. Another project, Save Our Sounds, a joint Library of Congress/Smithsonian Institution initiative funded by Save America's Treasures, is busy preserving original recordings—from Martin Luther King, Jr.'s famous "I have a dream" speech to Woody Guthrie's long version of "This Land is Your Land," a recording that, until recently, people thought had never been made at all.

The efforts I've been part of at the Library of Congress and Smithsonian are part of a global movement to restore, preserve, and disseminate the riches of the world's musical history. The Berlin Phonogramm-Archiv, the granddaddy of world music collections, celebrated its hundredth anniversary in 2000 and is in the forefront of European efforts to digitize and to repatriate music collections. With the help of UNESCO and other international agencies, the major collecting institutions, from older European centers like Vienna and Paris to newer archives established in Asia and the Pacific, are now part of a global sound network. We can look forward to a future when indexes and information about the digital holdings of these collections will all be available on the Web. Perhaps it will lead to a new form of musical exchange, like the digital-transfer, tape trading that exists among the Dead Heads.

When you go out into the field and make recordings and bring them back as your own, you've stolen someone else's property. It's theft, and it's been one of the great crimes of the century. But we can now make some kind of restitution for that by giving the credit back to the rightful creators, as well as giving back any monies earned by the sale or reproduction of the music. —Mickey Hart

In 2001, by an Act of Congress, the National Digital Registry was formed and Dr. Billington asked me to serve on the Board. The Board's task is to identify and preserve the most endangered and culturally significant recordings in any archive in the world. Now, at last, there is recognition that the musics of a people are cultural legacies of great worth and fragility.

If these recordings are not preserved, they will be lost forever. Our generation will be held accountable for the future of this legacy, because we are the first generation with the ability to preserve recordings indefinitely using digital technology. Just as we try to protect our forests and rivers and the air we breathe, we have to protect our musical heritage as a necessity of life. Music is one of humanity's greatest inventions—a repository of its dreams, histories, and hopes. Without our voices and musics we are no longer fully human. To allow such loss is unacceptable.

It is my hope that someday we will have enough money and enough support for this kind of recording and preservation. With ever improving and increasingly affordable digital technologies, we could give people everywhere access to all of the world's music, so that the dreams of the early songcatchers would live on in the music they preserved.

Mickey performs in Boston during the
Planet Drum tour in 1991.

FURTHER READING

Baldwin, Neil. *Edison: Inventing the Century*. Chicago: University of Chicago Press, 2001.

Bartis, Peter. *Folklife and Fieldwork: A Layman's Introduction to Field Techniques*. Washington, D.C.: Publications of the American Folklife Center, No. 3, Revised and expanded edition, 1990.

Bartók, Peter. *My Father*. Homassa, Fl.: Bartók Records, 2002.

Bartz, Gregory F. and Timothy J. Cooley, eds. *Shadows in the Field: New Perspectives for Fieldwork in Ethnomusicology*. New York: Oxford University Press, 1977.

Berlin, Gabriele and Artur Simon, eds. *Music Archiving in the World*. Berlin: Verlag für Wissenschaft und Bildung, 2002.

Bird, John. *Percy Grainger*. Oxford: Oxford University Press, 1999.

Blacking, John. *How Musical is Man?* Seattle: University of Washington Press, 1973.

——— *'A Commonsense View of All Music': Reflections on Percy Grainger's Contribution to Ethnomusicology and Music Education*. Cambridge: Cambridge University Press, 1987.

Bowles, Paul. *Without Stopping*. New York: Ecco Press, 1972.

Brady, Erika. *A Spiral Way: How the Phonograph Changed Ethnography*. Jackson: University Press of Mississippi, 1999.

Brown, Dee. *Bury My Heart at Wounded Knee*. New York: Henry Holt & Co., 2001.

Boulton, Laura. *The Music Hunter: The Autobiography of a Career*. Garden City, N.Y.: Doubleday, 1969.

Carpenter, Edmund. *Oh, What a Blow that Phantom Gave Me!* New York: Bantam, 1974.

Chanan, Michael. *Repeated Takes: A Short History of Recording and Its Effects on Music*. London: Verso, 1995.

Chernoff, John Miller. *African Rhythm and African Sensibility: Aesthetics and Social Action in African Musical Idioms*. Chicago: University of Chicago Press, 1979.

Clifford, James and George E. Marcus. *Writing Culture: The Poetics and Politics of Ethnography*. Berkeley: University of California Press, 1986.

Cole, Douglas. *Franz Boas: The Early Years*. Seattle: University of Washington Press, 1999.

Daniélou, Alain. *The Way to the Labyrinth: Memories of East and West*. New York: New Directions, 1987.

Dorson, Richard, ed. *Handbook of American Folklore*. Bloomington: Indiana University Press, 1983.

Dunaway, David King. *How Can I Keep From Singing: Pete Seeger*. New York: McGraw-Hill, 1982.

Ellingson, Ter. *The Myth of the Noble Savage*. Berkeley: University of California Press, 2001.

Ethnomusicology: Journal of the Society for Ethnomusicology.

Feld, Steven. *Sound and Sentiment: Birds, Weeping, Poetics, and Song in Kaluli Expression*. 2d ed. Philadelphia: University of Pennsylvania Press, 1982.

——— *Music Grooves*. Chicago: University of Chicago Press, 1995.

Friedman, Sam H., ed. *The Rebel Song Book*. New York: Rand School Press, 1935.

Garland Press. *The Garland Encyclopedia of World Music*. New York: Garland, 1998–2002. 10 Volumes.

Goldstein, Kenneth S. *A Guide for Fieldworkers in Folklore*. Hatsboro, PA: American Folklore Society, 1964.

Goldsmith, Peter D. *Making People's Music: Moe Asch and Folkways Records*. Washington, D.C.: Smithsonian Institution Press, 2000.

Halsey, Steven. *The Life and Music of Béla Bartók*. New York: Oxford University Press, 1964,

Hinsley, Curtis M., Jr. *Savages and Scientists: The Smithsonian Institution and the Development of American Anthropology 1846–1910*. Washington, D.C.: Smithsonian Institution Press, 1981.

Hitchcock, H. Wiley, ed. *The Phonograph and Our Musical Life*. New York: Brooklyn College, 1980. I.S.A.M. Monographs: No. 14

Hofmann, Charles, ed. *Frances Densmore and American Indian Music: A Memorial Volume*. New York: Museum of the American Indian, Heye Foundation, 1968.

Hood, Mantle. *The Ethnomusicologist*. 2d ed. Kent, OH: Kent State University Press, 1982.

Howard, Jane. *Margaret Mead: A Life*. New York: Simon and Schuster, 1984.

Hymes, Dell, ed. *Reinventing Anthropology*. New York: Vintage, 1974.

Jackson, Bruce. *Fieldwork*. Urbana: University of Illinois Press, 1987.

Judd, N.M. *The Bureau of American Ethnology: A Partial History*. Norman, OK: University of Oklahoma Press, 1968.

Karpeles, Maud, ed. *The Collection of Folk Music and Other Ethnomusicological Materials: A Manual for Fieldworkers*. London: International Folk Music Council, 1958.

Klein, Joe. *Woody Guthrie: A Life*. New York: Knopf, 1980.

Lomax, Alan. *Cantometrics: A Method in Musical Anthropology*. Berkeley: University of California Extension Media Center, 1976.

———. *Folk Song Style and Culture*. Washington: American Association for the Advancement of Science, 1968.

———. *The Land Where the Blues Began*. New York: The New Press, 1993.

Lortat-Jacob, Bernard. *Sardinian Chronicles*. Chicago: University of Chicago Press, 1995.

Mark, Joan. *A Stranger in Her Native Land: Alice Fletcher and the American Indians*. Lincoln: University of Nebraska Press, 1988.

McEntyre, Nancy C., ed. *Discourse in Ethnomusicology 3: Essays in Honor of Frank J. Gillis*. Bloomington: Ethnomusicology Publications Group, 1991.

McNally, Dennis. *A Long, Strange Trip: The Inside History of the Grateful Dead*. New York: Broadway Books, 2002.

McPhee, Colin. *A House in Bali*. New York: John Day, 1946.

———. *A Club of Small Men: A Story of Bali*. New York: John Day, 1948.

Mead, Margaret. *Letters From the Field: 1925-1975*. New York: Harper & Row, 1977.

Myers, Helen, ed. *Ethnomusicology: An Introduction*. New York: Norton, 1992.

———. *Ethnomusicology: Historical and Regional Studies*. New York: Norton, 1993.

Nettl, Bruno. *The Study of Ethnomusicology: 29 Issues and Concepts*. Urbana: University of Illinois Press, 1983.

Nettl, Bruno and Philip Bohlman, eds. *Comparative Musicology and the Anthropology of Music: Essays on the History of Ethnomusicology*. Chicago: University of Chicago Press, 1991.

Pescatello, Ann M. *Charles Seeger: A Life in American Music*. Pittsburgh: University of Pittsburgh Press, 1992.

Porterfield, Nolan. *Last Cavalier: The Life and Times of John A. Lomax*. Urbana: University of Illinois Press, 1996.

Post, Jennifer C., Mary Russell Bucknum and Laurel Sercombe. *A Manual for Documentation, Fieldwork, and Preservation*. Bloomington: Society for Ethnomusicology, 1994.

Rydell, Robert W., John E. Findling, and Kimberly D. Pelle, *Fair America*. Smithsonian Institution: Washington, D.C., 2000.

Sadie, Stanley, ed. *The New Grove Dictionary of Music and Musicians*. 2d ed. New York: Grove, 2001. 29 volumes. The standard reference work for music, musicology, ethnomusicology.

Seeger, Anthony and Louise Spear, eds. *Early Field Recordings*. Bloomington: Indiana University Press, 1987.

Shelemay, Kay Kaufman, ed. *The Garland Library of Readings in Ethnomusicology*. New York: Garland, 1990. 7 volumes of key essays in the field.

——— *A Song of Longing: An Ethiopian Journey*. Urbana: University of Illinois Press, 1991.

Silber, Irwin. *Songs America Voted By*. Harrisburg: Stackpole Press, 1988.

Stocking, George W. Jr., ed. *Observers Observed. Essays on Ethnographic Fieldwork*. Madison: University of Wisconsin Press, 1983.

Taussig, Michael. *Shamanism, Colonialism, and the Wild Man: A Study in Terror and Healing*. Chicago: University of Chicago Press, 1987.

Van Maanen, John. *Tales of the Field: On Writing Ethnography*. Chicago: University of Chicago Press, 1988.

Welch, Walter L., Burt, Leah, and Frow, George. *From Tinfoil to Stereo*. Gainesville: University Press of Florida, 1994.

Wilgus, D. K. *Anglo-American Folksong Scholarship Since 1898*. New Brunswick, NJ: Rutgers University Press, 1959.

Yurchenco, Henrietta. *Around the World in 80 Years: A Memoir*. Point Richmond, CA: MRI Press, 2002.

Index

Acknowledgements

INSPIRATIONS

The Good ol' GRATEFUL DEAD, who nurtured my enthusiasm for the world's music and allowed me the opportunity to explore the wild side of sound.

USTAD ALLA RAKHA, who showed me the connection between fluid rhythm made on a drum and the rhythm worlds all around us, in nature, in machines, everywhere there's life.

TITO PUENTE, who propelled my dance ritual with lightning bolt power. His music touched a place in me that still lives and grows.

DAN HEALY, who started me off on the trail of good sound. He was my teacher and mentor in the spirit of field recording.

OWSLEY STANLEY, who first introduced to me the idea of a "soundscape."

THEY MADE IT HAPPEN

KAREN KOSTYAL, my co-writer, who took an amazing amount of material and boiled it down to its essence. She brought order to my chaos. Without her, this book could not have been written. I salute you!

STEVEN FELD, a valuable ally in the formative stages of this work who continued to keep me on course over the many months of researching, writing, and editing.

FREDRIC LIEBERMAN, as always a major resource and fine eye in the editing stages. Over the years we have researched and written three books together. Fred is always a wealth of information with sensitive insight.

DR. JAMES BILLINGTON, Librarian of Congress, keeper of dreams, who greatly assisted me in the stacks, giving me unlimited and far-reaching access to the amazing information buried deep within the Library of Congress.

The following scholars graciously gave their insight, experience, and time helping me get it right.

PETER BARTÓK, OLIVER BERLINER, DIETER CHRISTENSEN, ELIZABETH COHEN, H. WILEY HITCHCOCK, BILL KLINGER, DAVID LEWISTON, NEIL MAKEN, DAVID MCALLESTER, TOM MILLER, BARRY OULD, ANTHONY SEEGER, NICK SPITZER, RUTH STONE, JOE WILSON, TOM VENNUM, HENRIETTA YURCHENCO, HUGO ZEMP

The 360° PRODUCTIONS staff

HOWARD COHEN, LOIS COHEN, TOM FLYE, ROSA ROBLES, RICARDO RAMIREZ, MARY ANN WADE

WARRIORS FOR SOUND PRESERVATION

Peggy Bulger, Director, American Folklife Center, and its staff, advisors, and friends at the Library of Congress, who tirelessly transfer recordings to the digital domain for future listeners.

KEN BILBY, SAM BRYLAWSKI, DORIS CRAIG, JENNIFER CUTTING, MAX DERRICKSON, KAY SHELEMAY, JUDITH GRAY, JOE HICKERSON, ALAN JABBOUR, MORTON MARKS, LYNN PEDIGO, MICHAEL TAFT

Friends who have assisted me in moving smoothly through the bureaucracies of Washington, D.C.

JONATHAN ADELSTEIN, DIANE BLAGMAN, RICHARD KURIN, ATESH SONNEBORN

I would also like to acknowledge:

All the folks at GRATEFUL DEAD PRODUCTIONS with special thanks to RAM.

ROD, DENNIS MCNALLY, JEFFREY NORMAN, DAVID LEMIEUX, EILEEN LAW, and CAMERON SEARS.

DON ROSE and ARTHUR MANN, great visionaries and founders of the Rykodisc CD label, home of the World series and Endangered Music Project. Thanks for giving all my musical passions a home.

CHERYL MCENANEY, who single-handedly introduced many record stores and mainstream music buyers, as well as anyone who would listen, to the treasure of the world's music.

JOHN AND HELEN MEYER, designers of the best speakers in the world, in front of which I spend many hours each day.

Photo Credits

DISCOGRAPHY

PUBLICATIONS BY MICKEY HART

Drumming at the Edge of Magic, with Jay Stevens and Fredric Lieberman. Grateful Dead Books

Planet Drum, with Fredric Lieberman and D.A. Sonneborn. Grateful Dead Books

Spirit into Sound: The Magic of Music, with Fredric Lieberman. Grateful Dead Books

RECORDINGS

By Mickey Hart:

Numerous recordings with the Grateful Dead between 1967 and the present.

Aladdin (Rabbit Ears 74041-72000-2)

At the Edge (RCD–10124/RACS).

Däfos. With Airto Moreira, and Flora Purim. (RCD 10108/RACS).

The Best of Mickey Hart: Over the Edge and Back (DVDA10494).

Music to Be Born By. With Taro Hart. (RCD 20112/RACS)

Mickey Hart's Mystery Box (RCD 10338/RAC).

Planet Drum (RCD 10206/RACS).

Planet Drum. Supralingua (RCD 10396/RAC).

Planet Drum. Indoscrub DVD (RDVD 5-1059)

Rolling Thunder (GDCD 40112)

Spirit into Sound (GDCD 4071)

The WORLD series:

The Diga Rhythm Band. *Diga* (RCD 10101/RACS).

Dzintars Latvian Women's Choir. *Songs of Amber* (RACD 10130/RACS).

Hariprasad Chaurasia and Zakir Hussain. *Venu* (RCD 20128).

Hamza el Din. *Eclipse* (RCD 10103/RACS).

The Golden Gate Gypsy Orchestra. *The Travelling Jewish Wedding* (RACD 10105/RASC).

The Gyuto Monks Tantric Choir. *Freedom Chants from the Roof of the World* (RCD 20113/RACS).

Ustad Sultan Kahn. *Sarangi: The Music of India* (RCD10104/RACS).

Babatunde Olatunji. *Drums of Passion: The Beat* (RCD 10107/RACS).

Babatunde Olatunji. *Drums of Passion: The Invocation* (RCD 10102/RACS).

The Rhythm Devils. *The Apocalypse Now Sessions* (RCD 10109/RACS).

Various Artists. *American Warriors: Songs for Indian Veterans* (RCD 10370/RAC).

Various Artists. *Around the World (For a Song)* (RCD00217/RACA)

Various Artists. *Honor the Earth Powwow* (RCD 10199/RACS).

Various Artists. *Living Art, Sounding Spirit: The Bali Sessions* (RCD 10449).

Various Artists. *Music of Upper and Lower Egypt* (RCD 10106/RACS).

Various Artists. *Utom: Summoning the Spirit, Music in the T'boli Heartland* (RCD 10402/RAC).

Various Artists. *Voices of the Rain Forest* (RACD 10173/RACS).

Library of Congress Endangered Music Project:

The Library of Congress Endangered Music Project *L.H. Corrêa de Azevedo: Music of Ceará and Minas Gerais* (RCD10404).

The Library of Congress Endangered Music Project *The Discoteca Collection: Missão de Pesquisas* (RCD10403).

The Library of Congress Endangered Music Project *Music for the Gods: The Fahnestock South Sea* (RCD10315).

The Library of Congress Endangered Music Project *The Spirit Cries: Music from the Rainforests of South America and the Caribbean* (RCD 10250).

The Library of Congress Endangered Music Project *The Arthur Alberts Collection: More Tribal, Folk, and Café Music of West Africa* (RCD 10401)

The Library of Congress Endangered Music Project.
The Yoruba and Dahomean Collection: Orishas Across the Ocean (RCD 10405).

OTHER RECORDINGS AND FILMS

'Are'are Panpipe Ensembles (Le Chant du Monde LDX 274961.62, Harmonia Mundi)

'Are'are Intimate and Ritual Music (Le Chant du Monde CNR 274963, Harmonia Mundi)

The Gyuto Monks Tantric Choir. (WD-2001)

Cohen, Ronald and Dave Samuelson, 1996. *Songs for Political Action: Folkmusic, Topical Songs and the American Left 1926-1953.* 121-page book and 10 Compact Discs (Bear Family Records) BCD 15720JL

Kodo. *Mondo Head* (Red Ink WK 56111)

Masques Dan, Côte-d'Ivoire. (Ocora C 580048, Harmonia Mundi)

Place, Jeff and Ronald Cohen 2000. *The Best of Broadside: Anthems of the American Underground 1962-1988.* 5-CD set and 158-page book. Washington DC: Smithsonian Folkways Recordings SFW

Sammy Hagar. *Marching to Mars* (Universal)

The Song of Harmonics. 1989. Documentary film on Mongolian overtone singing. Distribution: CNRS Audiovisuel, 1 place Aristide Briand , F - 92190 Meudon.

The Masters of the Balafon. 2001-02. Documentary series of 4 films about the xylophone music of the Senufo people, Côte d'Ivoire. Available from the distributor <Suporxao@free.fr>

ABOUT THE AUTHORS

MICKEY HART is best known for his three decades with the Grateful Dead and for his incorporation of percussion instruments and sounds from around the world in the band's repertoire.

In addition to his own activities as a musician and recording artist, Hart produced the acclaimed series of recordings known as THE WORLD which made a vast range of music from around the globe available to a wide audience. Hart's passion for the world's music led him to many great teachers and collaborators, including his partners on the album *Planet Drum*, which earned the first Grammy Award for Best World Music Album in 1991.

Over the years, Mickey Hart has become an eloquent spokesperson and advocate for the restoration and preservation of the world's aural treasures. In recognition of his work in this field, Hart was appointed to the Board of Trustees of the American Folklife Center, as well as the National Recorded Sound Preservation Board at the Library of Congress, where he works on the digitization and preservation of the Library's vast collections. He also works with the leadership committee of the Save Our Sounds organization in spearheading efforts to preserve audio recordings of great cultural and historical value.

Hart's lifelong fascination with rhythm, the history of percussion, and music has been documented in three books: *Drumming at the Edge of Magic* (with Jay Stevens and Fredric Lieberman); *Planet Drum* (with Fredric Lieberman and D.A. Sonneborn); and *Spirit into Sound: The Magic of Music* (with Fredric Lieberman).

K.M. KOSTYAL has written frequently on historical topics and world travel. Her books include *Trial by Ice: A Photobiography of Sir Ernest Shackleton; Peoples of the World* (ed.), *Cradle and Crucible: History and Faith in the Middle East* (ed.); *Stonewall Jackson: A Life Portrait*; and *Virginia: The Spirit of America*. She lives in Alexandria, Virginia.

CREDITS

SONGCATCHERS
IN SEARCH OF THE WORLD'S MUSIC
MICKEY HART with K.M. KOSTYAL

Published by the National Geographic Society

JOHN M. FAHEY, JR., *President and Chief Executive Officer*
GILBERT M. GROSVENOR, *Chairman of the Board*
NINA D. HOFFMAN, *Executive Vice President*

Prepared by the Book Division

KEVIN MULROY, *Vice President and Editor-in-Chief*
CHARLES KOGOD, *Illustrations Director*
MARIANNE R. KOSZORUS, *Design Director*

Staff for this Book

LISA LYTTON, *Editor*
PAT DANIELS, *Text Editor*
MARGARET JOHNSON, *Illustrations Editor*
MARILYN GIBBONS, *Illustrations Editor*
MELANIE DOHERTY DESIGN, *Art Director*
TINA BESA, *Designer*
GARY COLBERT, *Production Director*
SHARON BERRY, *Illustrations Assistant*
CAROLINDA E. AVERITT, *Consulting Editor*

Manufacturing and Quality Control

CHRISTOPHER A. LIEDEL, *Chief Financial Officer*
PHILLIP L. SCHLOSSER, *Managing Director*
VINCENT P. RYAN, *Manager*

One of the world's largest nonprofit scientific and educational organizations, the National Geographic Society was founded in 1888 "for the increase and diffusion of geographic knowledge." Fulfilling this mission, the Society educates and inspires millions every day through its magazines, books, television programs, videos, maps and atlases, research grants, the National Geographic Bee, teacher workshops, and innovative classroom materials. The Society is supported through membership dues, charitable gifts, and income from the sale of its educational products. This support is vital to National Geographic's mission to increase global understanding and promote conservation of our planet through exploration, research, and education.

For more information, please call 1-800-NGS LINE (647-5463) or write to the following address:

NATIONAL GEOGRAPHIC SOCIETY
1145 17th Street N.W.
Washington, D.C. 20036-4688 U.S.A.

Visit the Society's Web site at
www.nationalgeographic.com.

For more information on *Songcatchers* and the World's music, please visit Mickey Hart's Web site at mickeyhart.net.

Library of Congress Cataloging-in-Publication Data

Hart, Mickey
    Songcatchers : in search of the world's music /
    Mickey Hart with K.M. Kostyal.
            p.   cm.
    Includes bibliographical references (p.) and index.
    ISBN 0-7922-4107-X
    1. World music—History and criticism.
    2. Ethnomusicology. I. Kostyal, K. M., 1951-II. Title.

    ML3545.H25 2003
    780'.9—dc21
                                        2003045901